Kathy Schrock's
Every Day of the School Year Series

Daily Celebration Activities:

February through June

Midge Frazel

A Publication of Linworth Learning

Linworth Publishing, Inc.
Worthington, Ohio

Published by Linworth Publishing, Inc.
480 East Wilson Bridge Road, Suite L
Worthington, Ohio 43085

ISBN 1-58683-107-0

5 4 3 2

✧ Table of Contents ✧

FEBRUARY

MARCH

❖ Table of Contents ❖

APRIL

MAY

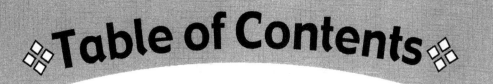

Table of Contents

JUNE

About the Author

Midge Frazel is a consultant specializing in educational technology. She designs and develops workshops for teachers to help them learn how to manage computer technology hardware and software productively and to integrate technology into the classroom curriculum. Readers can use Midge's Home Page <http://www.midgefrazel.net> as a classroom, library media center, or public library resource. She may be reached at *midgef@midgefrazel.net*. Midge has co-authored two books with Kathy Schrock and authored another available only in electronic format.

Midge celebrates National Blonde Day on July 9 and her favorite holiday falls on October 31.

Acknowledgements

I would like to thank the teachers who contributed their own classroom activities to celebrate. They are Kathy Wasik of Bridgewater, Massachusetts; Debbie Zakowski of Seekonk, Massachusetts; Gayle Bradbury of Somerset, Massachusetts; and last, my daughter, Heather Frazel, of Newton, Massachusetts. They gave freely of their precious time. These classroom-tested lessons are the heart of this book.

Thanks also to Kathy Schrock, whose encouragement and patience during this project kept me sane. Also, to my husband Steve for seeing nothing but my back at my computer for months! A special thank you to the librarians of the Bridgewater Public Library for their help with the print resources and to my co-workers for the technical help I needed as I went along.

There is so much in life to celebrate—at home, at school, at work, and in the world. I'd like to celebrate the lives of those who perished in the attack on America on September 11, 2001. Freedom is the ultimate celebration.

A Word From ❖ Kathy Schrock ❖

Welcome to the Every Day of the School Year Series! As an educator, library media specialist, and now technology administrator, I know how important it is for the classroom teacher to extend the learning experiences in the classroom. With the current focus on standards-based teaching, learning, and assessment, I felt it was important to supply classroom teachers and library media specialists with activities which directly support the curriculum, but, at the same time, allow for creative teachers to provide supplementary and extension activities for their students.

The activities in this series are varied in scope, but all of them provide practical tips, tricks, ideas, activities and units. Many of the activities include related print and Internet sites, which are easily collected by the classroom teacher before engaging in the activity. There are handouts, worksheets, and much more throughout the books, too. In my job as technology administrator for a school district, I am often able to plan lessons with teachers and visit classrooms to observe the teaching of the lesson. In addition, as the creator and maintainer, since 1995, of Kathy Schrock's Guide for Educators (http://discoveryschool.com/schrockguide/), a portal of categorized Web sites for teachers, I often receive e-mail from teachers who are searching for practical, creative, and easy-to-implement activities for the classroom. I hope this series provides just the impetus for you to stretch and enhance your textbook, lesson, and standards-based unit by use of these activities!

If you have any titles you would like to see added to the series, or would like to author yourself, drop me a note at kathy@kathyschrock.net

Kathy Schrock

How to Use this Book

The activities featured in this book give teachers the opportunity to start each day with a celebration, or to enrich their curriculum with an integrated celebration activity. Daily lessons can be enhanced by introducing interesting historical, cultural, literary and amusing events to spark students' interest in the world around them and to create excitement about a particular subject area. Melding the past with the present, and adding a splash of the future as a daily introductory event, can make a difference in the lives of your students.

For centuries, every nation, culture and society has set aside days for festivals, fiestas and thanksgiving. The celebrations presented here will help students understand and respect the varied customs and traditions that are the foundation of our American culture.

Art, music, physical education, science, history, literature, mathematics and geography all contain events to celebrate, and are each represented in this book. Many of the activities are interdisciplinary, which allow the integration of science, mathematics and the arts into language and social studies based lessons. This type of learning can connect many disciplines within the confines of a single school day and provide students with a basis for the deeper learning that happens in later grades.

The activities have been divided into monthly sections to fit easily into lesson plan preparations. As you plan, keep in mind the needs and ability levels of your students. Take notes on this year's experiences, considering your students level of interest, to help you plan for next year. This book contains late winter, spring and early summer activities, from February through June. A companion book has celebration activities that cover September through January.

Journal writing is promoted as a central focus, to develop the critical thinking, organization and personal reflection skills essential for effective communication. Project-based work, both individual and teamed, is suggested as well as methods of effective presentation of the material learned. Rich with links to literature in print to promote success in reading, these activities also make connections to information found on the Internet to celebrate the best use of technology and print resources.

Tips for Using the Internet in the Classroom:

- If you have a one-computer classroom, assign a team of students to work on the computer, using the prepared Web site resources as a guide. Each month, a new team can be "incharge."

- If you have a computer lab available, pick celebrations that fit into the lab appointment schedule.

- If you only have online access at one computer or have to use your personal home computer, mark those activities that fit your curriculum plan and concentrate on the technology integration at that point.

Following the theme of celebrations, the lessons in this book have strong ties to the national standards in language arts, social studies, and foreign languages. As you choose a daily event to celebrate, use the guidelines listed here to match the benchmarks of your individual state standards and frameworks.

How to Use this Book

In kindergarten through grade three, activities connect to the national standards in social studies revolving around the celebrations of home and community. By combining these ideals with the suggested readings and Web sites, and with the introduction of journal writing, these standards can be tied to NCTE standards one and five.

For students in grades four and five, continuing with the benchmarks established in the earlier grades, links can be made to the celebration of important dates in American history and the celebrations of other cultures. As students begin to conduct research, gather, evaluate and synthesize information, NCTE standard seven is met. Using technology as a process for effective communication ties to NCTE standard eight. Students will also be involved in NCTE standards eleven and twelve, which connect journal writing, reflection, and creative thinking to reading, writing and communication.

We all look forward to celebrations, and by using these lessons in the classroom, we can engage, motivate and inspire young learners.

Let's begin each school day with a celebration!

February

Activity 1:
Celebrate Wild Bird Feeding Month

Subject: Science

Grade level: K to 5

Celebrate the lives of wild birds in this month of February by learning to use student journals as scientific data recording tools. Wild bird feeding, watching, identifying and recording can teach the essential skills of science journaling. Students will probably enjoy this project so much they will want to set up bird feeders at home.

Activity Title:
Wild Birds

Materials:

Outside classroom window bird feeder, field guides for students on birds, Web site access, birdseed, student journals, Reproducible Activity 1: Journal Cover, Reproducible Activity 1: Inside Cover: List of Holidays

Procedure:

Purchase an inexpensive hanging bird feeder and seed, and place it outside the classroom window. Use Web sites or print field guides for students to use in identification of the birds that visit the feeder.

Brainstorm with the students the journal activity of recording field data. Assign students days to observe, weather condition recording, and care of the feeder by grouping the students into teams.

Evaluation:

Students will learn to use their student journals as a science tool for the observation and recording of data.

Resources:
The Life of Birds
    <http://www.pbs.org/lifeofbirds/>
Project Feederwatch
    <http://birds.cornell.edu/pfw/>
Watchlist 4 Kids: Bird Recording Template
    <http://www.audubon.org/bird/watch/kids/template.html>

Activity 1: Journal Cover

Activity 1: Inside Cover: List of Holidays

Commonly Celebrated Holidays

New Year's Day
Inauguration Day
Martin L. King Day
Abraham Lincoln's Birthday
President's Day
George Washington's Birthday
Arbor Day
Mother's Day
Memorial Day
Flag Day
Father's Day
Independence Day
Labor Day
Columbus Day
Veterans Day
Thanksgiving Day
Christmas Day

Date Celebrated

January 1
January 20 (every four years)
Third Monday in January
February 12
Third Monday in February
February 22
Last Friday in April
Second Sunday in May
Last Monday in May
June 14
Third Sunday in June
July 4
First Monday in September
Second Monday in October
November 11
Fourth Thursday in November
December 25

Often Celebrated Holidays

Groundhog Day
St. Valentine's Day
April Fool's day
Halloween
St. Patrick's Day
Cinco de Mayo
Earth Day

Date Celebrated

February 2
February 14
April 1
October 31
March 17
May 5
April 22

Other Holidays

Chinese New Year
Passover
Easter
Yom Kippur
Chanukah
Kwanzaa

Enter Date Celebrated This Year

_____
_____
_____
_____
_____
_____
_____
_____

Personal Holidays/Celebrations

Birthday

_____
_____
_____
_____

_____
_____
_____
_____

Celebrate Groundhog Day

Subject: Science, Art, Writing
Grade level: 3 to 4

> Celebrate Groundhog Day on February 2 by learning facts and fables about the famous Phil, the groundhog.

Activity Title:
Winter Shadow

Materials:

Web site access, local television morning or noon news report, Reproducible Activity 2: KWL Graphic Organizer

Procedure:

Photocopy Reproducible 2: KWL Graphic Organizer and distribute one to each student to begin learning about Groundhog Day. Is the story of the famous groundhog fact or fiction?

Use the Web sites to learn about groundhogs, the spring equinox, and shadows.

Ask students to create their own news report about this day and compare it to the real news of the day.

Evaluation:

Students will learn to distinguish fact from fiction about Groundhog Day

Resources:

Levine, Abby. *Gretchen Groundhog: It's Your Day!* Morton Grove, IL: Albert Whitman, 1998.
Day of the Shadow
        <http://www.geocities.com/Heartland/7134/Shadow/groundhog.htmGroundhog Day>
        <http://www.groundhog.org/activities/>
Facts about Groundhogs from Cornell University
        <http://www.news.cornell.edu/Chronicle/96/2.1.96/facts.html>
Groundhog Activity Sheets to Print
        <http://www.geocities.com/athens/thebes/9893/groundhogprint.html>

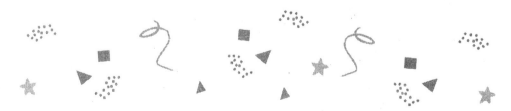

Activity 2: KWL Graphic Organizer

Name _____

Know	Want to Know	Learned

Name _____

Know	Want to Know	Learned

Celebrate the One Hundredth Day of School

Subject: Math

Grade level: K to 2

> Celebrate the One-Hundredth Day of School! Many early childhood classrooms begin the countdown to this day on the first day of school, and it is a favorite part of the math curriculum.

Activity Title:
 Big Number

Materials:

Web site access, suggested readings

Procedure:

The Web shines with activities, ideas, and class projects to tie the number 100 into every aspect of the curriculum. Some schools have a whole school event with the older students helping the younger students with counting and estimation. Team with another teacher of a higher grade level to have those students help in your classroom. Even the youngest students can count 100 pennies in honor of Abraham Lincoln's birthday.

Evaluation:

Students will learn about the number 100 by participating in a hands-on math activity.

Resources:

Cuyler, Margaret. *100th Day Worries*. New York: Simon & Schuster Books for Young Readers, 2000.
Slate, Joseph. *Miss Bindergarten Celebrates 100th Day of Kindergarten*. New York: Dutton Children's Books, 1998.
Joan Holub's 300 Celebration Ideas
    <http://users.aol.com/a100thday/ideas.html>
Connecting Students: 100 Days
    <http://www.teleport.com/~dleahy/themes/hundred.htm>

Celebrate Laura Ingalls Wilder's Birthday

Subject: Social Studies, Reading

Grade level: 3 to 5

> Laura Ingalls Wilder was born on February 7, 1867. Her stories of her life as a pioneer child have brought this time in history into focus for all of us. Both boys and girls love these stories and long to hear more about her life.

Activity Title:

Time Line Journey

Materials:

Suggested reading, Web site access, map of the United States, encyclopedias and atlases (traditional print, CD-ROM, or Web-based)

Procedure:

Encourage students to learn more about this period of history by having them create a time line of the journeys of the Ingalls and Wilder families. Extend the activity by finding out what was happening in the world during the years of this author's life. Your public library may have more biographies of this author available for your students to use.

Evaluation:

Students will learn to create a time line of a favorite author's life.

Resources:

Anderson, William. *Laura Ingalls Wilder: A Biography*. New York: Harper Trophy, 1992.
Laura Ingalls Wilder Time line Activity
    <http://www.hoover.nara.gov/kids/liw/pioneering _intro.html>
    <http://www.hoover.nara.gov/education/liw/time line_activity.html>

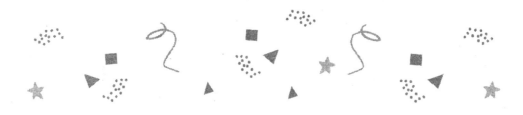

Celebrate Thomas Edison's Birthday

Subject: Science, Writing

Grade level: 4 to 5

Celebrate Thomas Alva Edison's Birthday on February 11 (1847) by learning about a man who is considered one of the world's greatest inventors.

Activity Title:
Perseverance

Materials:

Dictionaries, thesaurus, encyclopedias (traditional print, CD-ROM, or Web-based), books on Thomas Alva Edison, Web site access, student journals

Procedure:

Have students use dictionary skills to define "perseverance." Have them use a thesaurus to find synonyms for perseverance and write these in their journal.

Assign students to use their research skills in the school library media center or public library to create a list of Edison's inventions. How does invention require perseverance?

Evaluation:

Students will learn how hard work and determination play a part in the invention process.

Resources:

Murray, Peter. *Perseverance: The Story of Thomas Alva Edison*. Plymouth, MN: Child's World, 1996.
Edison Kids: Thomas Edison
    <http://www.edisonkids.com/heroexb/thomas.htm>
Edison National Historic Site
    <http://www.nps.gov/edis/home.htm>

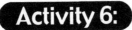
Celebrate Abraham Lincoln's Birthday

Subject: Social Studies

Grade level: K to 5

Use the whole month to study Lincoln, Washington, and Black History Month as a unit. Use the theme of honesty, truth, and freedom as a journal activity.

Activity Title:

Honesty

Materials:

Dictionaries and encyclopedias (traditional print, CD-ROM, or Web-based), books on the topic, Web site access

Procedure:

For younger students: Have the students use dictionary skills to define "honesty," "truth," and "freedom," and write those definitions in their journals. Create a poster or banner to hang in the classroom to define the spirit of February. They can use the suggested Web site to learn about the life of Lincoln.

For older students: Have students use the Lincoln's Famous Quotes Web site to learn what he had to say about honesty and freedom. They can start a study of the Emancipation Proclamation.

Evaluation:

Students will learn about Honest Abe as part of a month-long study.

Resources:

Weisbacher, Anne. *Abraham Lincoln.* Minneapolis: Abdo & Daughters, 2001.
Abraham Lincoln for Primary Children (younger students)
    <http://www.siec.k12.in.us/~west/proj/lincoln/>
Famous Quotes by Abraham Lincoln
    <http://showcase.netins.net/web/creative/lincoln/speeches/quotes.htm>

Celebrate Valentine's Day

Subject: Language Arts
Grade level: 2 to 5

> Celebrate February 14 with an activity that focuses on the unspoken, positive qualities that are in each one of us. This is a great way to give positive feedback and foster good feelings in each student. This activity works well for a classroom that has a student who does not celebrate holidays but can celebrate the special qualities of us all.

Activity Title:
Special Qualities by Kathleen Wasik

Materials:

Class list, light colored construction paper, pencil, ribbon or string, single-hole punch, Reproducible

Procedure:

Students will cut out hearts from a teacher-made tracer or use Reproducible Activity 7: Heart Tracer. All the hearts are the same size, approximately 2 to 2 1/2 inches. One is needed for each of the students and for the teacher.

Students will use the class list to write the individual names on one side of each heart.

On the other side the student will write a positive word or phrase about that student. Examples are "creative," "funny," "smart," "helpful," "imaginative," "good at sports." Students DO NOT sign their names.

Teacher/student may punch a hole at the top of each heart.

Students deliver the hearts to each student (students may have a paper caddy or mailbox ready for them).

Once all hearts have been delivered, the ribbon or string is put through the whole lot and tied at the end. It may be worn as a necklace.

Every student (and teacher too!) will have the chance to share what the others have written about him or her.

Evaluation:

Students will anonymously reveal to other students the positive qualities about these other students.

Resources:

Canfield, Jack, comp. *Chicken Soup for the Kid's Soul: 101 Stories of Courage, Hope and Laughter.* Deerfield Beach, FL: Health Communications, 1998.

Activity 7: Heart Tracer

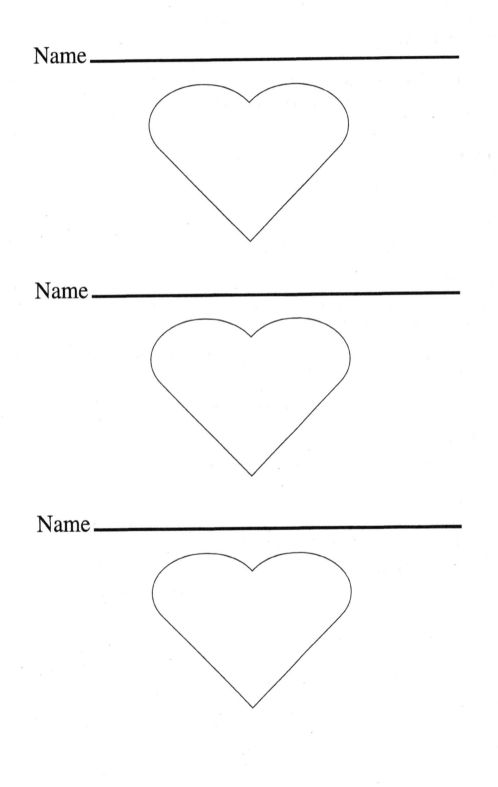

Name _____

Name _____

Name _____

Celebrate Snowflake Bentley's Birthday

Subject: Science

Grade level: 4 to 5

Celebrate the Birthday of Wilson Bentley (February 9, 1865), whose patience and persistence, combined with his knowledge of photography, earned him the title of the Snowflake Man.

Activity Title:

Snowflakes

Materials:

Suggested readings, Web site access

Procedure:

Begin a winter weather unit by learning about the life and work of "The Snowflake Man." The suggested book is a Caldecott Medal winner for 1989.

Use the Snowstorms in the Classroom Web site to learn about the science of snow, even if you live where there isn't any in February.

Add an art activity by making paper snowflakes to create a "blizzard" in your classroom.

Evaluation:

Students will learn about the science and beauty of snowflakes.

Resources:

Martin, Jacqueline Briggs. *Snowflake Bentley*. New York: Houghton Mifflin, 1998.
Snowflake Bentley Literature Guide by Nancy Polette
    <http://www.nancypolette.com/LitGuidesText/snowflake.htm>
Wilson A. Bentley: The Snowflake Man
    <http://snowflakebentley.com/>
Snowstorms in the Classroom
    <http://express.howstuffworks.com/quest.htm>

Celebrate National Cherry Month

Subject: Nutrition, Social Studies

Grade level: 3 to 4

February is National Cherry Month, so celebrate by not cutting down a cherry tree.

Activity Title:
Bowl of Cherries

Materials:

Encyclopedias (traditional print, CD-ROM, or Web-based), cherry desserts or juice, student journals

Procedure:

Ask the students about these sayings: "Life is just a bowl of cherries." "George Washington couldn't tell a lie; he cut down the cherry tree." "Life is the pits." This is a good day to find out about the growth, nutrition, taste, and fables of cherries.

Have students write about telling lies in their journals.

Evaluation:

Students will learn how fruit is grown, its place in our diet, and why George Washington's birthday is celebrated with cherries.

Resources:

Which Came First, the Cherry or the Pit?
    <http://www.cherrymkt.org/kidstuff/quickhist.htm>
The Papers of George Washington: Cherry Fables
    <http://www.virginia.edu/gwpapers/documents/weems/>

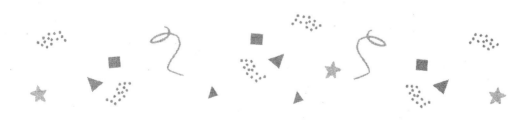

Activity 10:

Celebrate George Washington's Birthday (President's Day)

Subject: Social Studies
Grade level: 5

Celebrate President's Day by learning about the lives and work of two of our favorite Presidents.

Activity Title:
Truth

Materials:

Reproducible Activity 10: Venn Diagram Graphic Organizer, Web site access, books, encyclopedias or other print resources on Lincoln and Washington

Procedure:

Divide the class into two groups and have one group research Washington and the other group research Lincoln. Use the three words, "Truth," "Honesty," and "Freedom" to describe the lives and philosophies of these men who shaped the America we know today.

Hand out Reproducible Activity 10: Venn Diagram Graphic Organizer for students to record their own research. Use the whiteboard to create a class Venn diagram depicting these three ideals.

Evaluation:

Students will compare and contrast the lives and philosophies of two important Presidents.

Resources:

George Washington Life and Times (K to 5)
    <http://www.virginia.edu/gwpapers/lesson/k5/index.html>
President's Day
    <http://score.rims.k12.ca.us/activity/presidentsday/>

Activity 10: Venn Diagram Graphic Organizer

Name _____

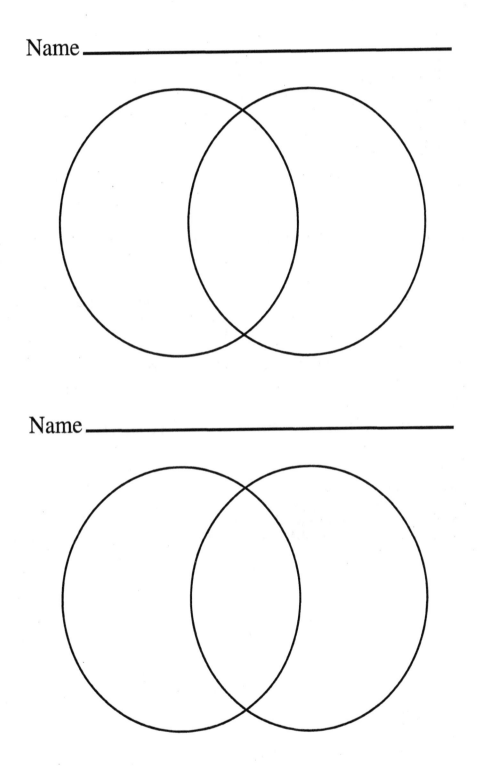

Name _____

Celebrate Black History Month

Subject: Social Studies

Grade level: 5

February is Black History Month. Honor Black American history and culture by devoting a week-long unit to the study of famous Black Americans.

Activity Title:

Freedom

Materials:

Web site access, juvenile biographies of selected Black Americans, student journals, art materials

Procedure:

Using the Web or print juvenile biographies, assign a person to a group of students to research. Have students use their student journals as an information-gathering tool. Include famous Black Americans from all walks of life and all areas of society on the list of choices.

This is a good time to introduce proper bibliographic citation formats.

Evaluation:

Students will use research skills to prepare informational posters or collages for classroom display.

Resources:

Notable African-Americans
    <http://www.kron.com/specials/blackhistory/home.html>
Education First: Black History Activities (teacher resource)
    <http://www.kn.pacbell.com/wired/BHM/AfroAm.html>

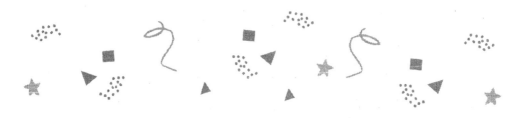

Activity 12:

Celebrate Grand Canyon National Park Anniversary

Subject: Science

Grade level: 4 to 5

> The Grand Canyon officially became a National Park on February 26, 1919. Begin a unit on geology in a big way

Activity Title:
Rocks and Layers

Materials:

Web site access

Procedure:

Learn about the geology of the Grand Canyon by using the Web. Even if you don't have classroom access to the Web, you can print these Web pages and use them as a resource in the classroom.

Extend this lesson into social studies by learning about the Native Americans in this area of the U.S. This celebration can be continued into March.

Evaluation:

Students will learn about geology by using the Grand Canyon as a resource.

Resources:

Peterson, David. *Grand Canyon National Park*. New York: Children's Press, 2001.
Grand Canyon National Park
   <http://www.nps.gov/grca/>
The Geology of the Grand Canyon
   <http://www.kaibab.org/gc/geology/gc_geol.htm>
Grand Canyon Rock Layers
   <http://www.kaibab.org/gc/geology/gc_layer.htm>

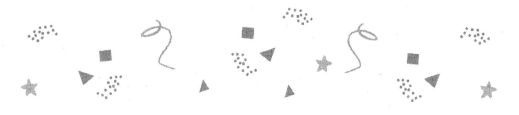

Celebrate Journal Writing Month

Subject: Journal Writing
Grade level: 1 to 5

Celebrate Journal Writing Month and have students learn more about journal writing.

Activity Title:
Journaling for Jobs

Materials:

Web site access, student journals, word processing software, tape recorder

Procedure:

Expand your student's knowledge with some examples of ships' logs, scientific notes and records, project planning journals, and spiritual journals. Students may enjoy keeping electronic journals or tape-recorded journals. Remind them that journaling is a life skill.

First graders can be introduced to journal writing and may use graphical representations of events or topics.

Evaluation:

Students will expand their knowledge of the types of journal writing.

Resources:

42Explore Topic: Journal Writing
      <http://eduscapes.com/42explore/journl.htm>
SCORE: Journaling Rubrics
      <http://www.sdcoe.k12.ca.us/score/actbank/tjournal.htm>

Celebrate American Heart Month

Subject: Health, Science

Grade level: 2 to 5

Celebrate American Heart Month by learning about the human heart, keeping fit, and eating properly to be "heart healthy."

Activity Title:
Cross Your Heart

Materials:

Books on heart anatomy, Web site access

Procedure:

Students can learn the biology of the human heart from many resources. Use one of these sources to learn the role the human heart plays in our life.

Brainstorm common phrases and sayings about our "emotional" hearts.

Invite the physical education teacher to provide cardiovascular exercise for the whole class (for example, jump rope or relay race).

Extend this lesson by learning about healthy eating, the role of fat in our diet, and how artificial hearts work.

Evaluation:

Students will learn the anatomy of the human heart and ways to keep it healthy.

Resources:

All About the Heart
    <http://kidshealth.org/kid/body/heart_SW.html>
The Heart: An Online Exhibit
    <http://sln.fi.edu/biosci/heart.html>

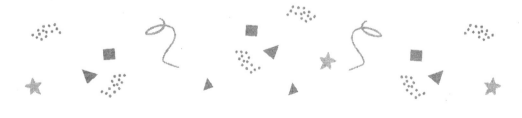

Celebrate Mardi Gras Day

Subject: Interdisciplinary

Grade level: 2 to 4

Celebrate Mardi Gras Day (Shrove or Fat Tuesday) by learning about this yearly event celebrated by feasting and merriment before the solemn events of Lent.

Activity Title:

Mask of Reflection

Materials:

Student journals, pancakes, Web site access

Procedure:

During Lent, many families teach their children important values of self-reflection by "giving up" something they like for a certain period of time. Celebrate this in the classroom by eating a breakfast or lunch of pancakes (a tradition of using up butter and eggs before Lenten meals) and making masks.

This is a good time to teach reflective journaling and its relation to character education.

Evaluation:

Students will learn about self-reflection and the lessons of giving up something they enjoy.

Resources:

Holidays on the Web: Mardi Gras
    <http://www.holidays.net/mardigras/index.htm>

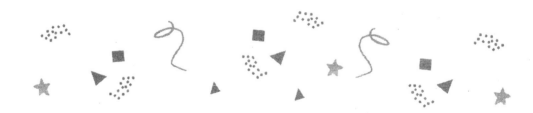

 March

Activity 16:

Celebrate Learning About Our National Parks Day

Subject: Social Studies

Grade level: 4 to 5

> Roar into March by investigating a Web-based adventure by the National Park Service.

Activity Title:
Landmarks

Materials:

Web site access, student journals

Procedure:

To enliven your student's knowledge about a famous place in the United States, take a trip to the computer lab to participate in an interactive, Web-based resource. During this adventure, your role as teacher is to guide students to the Web adventure, and to help with the reading of the text and the printing of the coloring pages.

Before the trip you should read the Teacher's Guide to help plan your experience.

Evaluation:

Students will learn to use a Web-based adventure to gather information about our national landmarks.

Resources:

The Great American Landmarks Adventure
    <http://www2.cr.nps.gov/pad/adventure/landmark.htm>
Teacher's Guide
    <http://www2.cr.nps.gov/pad/adventure/contents.htm>

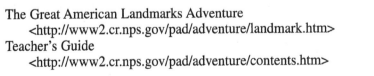

Celebrate Read Across America Day

Subject: Reading

Grade level: K to 5

Celebrate the Birthday of Dr. Seuss (March 2, 1904) by participating in a national reading program called Read Across America.

Activity Title:
Read Across America

Materials:

Web site access, community and school volunteer readers

Procedure:

Before the celebration, visit the Read Across America Web site to read the wealth of information available to help you with this celebration. There is a list of "to-do's" and reproducible handouts to print and use for the event.

If this is a district-wide celebration, develop a list of adults in the community who would like to participate in a classroom reading event. Create a list of curriculum-related books to be read as a suggestion for the participating grade levels. Lower elementary grade students may wish to celebrate Dr. Seuss's birthday with a reading of one of his books.

Contact your local news station or newspaper for publicity on this important celebration.

Evaluation:

Students will learn to value reading by sharing a book reading with an adult reader.

Resources:

Martin, Patricia Stone. *Dr. Seuss: We Love You!* Vero Beach, FL: Rourke Enterprises, 1997.
Read Across America
    <http://www.nea.org/readacross/index.html>
Dr. Seuss Activity Pages
    <http://abcteach.com/Reading/suess/suesstoc.htm>
Dr. Seuss's Seussville!
    <http://www.randomhouse.com/seussville/>

Celebrate the Iditarod Dog Sled Race Day

Subject: Interdisciplinary

Grade level: K to 5

Survival! Celebrate the annual running of Alaska's "Last Great Race" on the first Saturday of March with a whole school event! Rich with literature, science, math, history, and geography, this event brings with it the excitement of sports and a strong connection to the curriculum.

Activity Title:
Race to Survive!

Materials:
Web site access, books on the topic

Procedure:
Real-world connections are hard to come by in the elementary classroom. Use this project on a small scale by learning the historical significance and reading the associated literature, on a medium scale by creating a survival unit, or as a big project by using the Web to hear and see daily reports of the race.

Visit Jan Wong's excellent Web page resources for advice, projects that are classroom tested, and a full bibliography. This race is quite an experience!

Evaluation:
Students will experience an authentic connection to an annual event by reading, collecting data, viewing video, and listening to audio via the Web.

Resources:
The Iditarod Dog Sled Race
    <http://www.iditarod.com>
Iditarod 911 by Jan Wong
    <http://www.designperfect.com/iditarod>
Bibliography by Jan Wong
    <http://www.designperfect.com/iditarod/iditbook.htm>

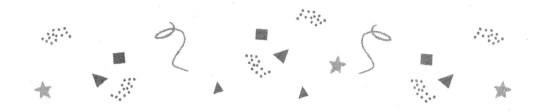

Celebrate Learning About Castles Day

Subject: Social Studies, Art
Grade level: 4 to 5

Whether you connect to a unit on King Arthur, Harry Potter, or fairy tales, March is a great time to celebrate learning about castles.

Activity Title:
Crafty Castles

Materials:

Art material, Web site access, books on the topic

Procedure:

Extend your previous study of medieval history by exploring resources in print and online to study the architecture of castles. Creating a classroom castle display is an engaging way to connect research to a hands-on activity.

Use student journals to take notes on castles from different periods of history. What would a castle of the future look like?

Evaluation:

Students will learn about castle architecture and apply it by designing a castle model.

Resources:

Blackwood, Gary L. *Life in a Medieval Castle*. San Diego, CA: Lucent Books, 2000.
Castle Discovery WebQuest
    <http://www.windarooss.qld.edu.au/Main_Pages/Castle_Webquest/welcome.htm>
Castles on the Web
    <http://www.castlesontheweb.com/>
Enchanted Learning Make a Castle
    <http://www.enchantedlearning.com/crafts/Boxcastle.shtml>

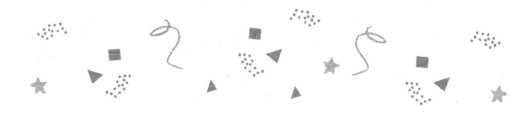

Celebrate Ladybug Day

Subject: Science, Reading

Grade level: K to 1

Celebrate the connection between science and reading by exploring a Web resource for teachers to enhance student instruction.

Activity Title:

Cool Insects

Materials:

Web site access, suggested reading list available during the project

Procedure:

Visit Susan Seagrave's excellent Web resource on ladybugs. Designed to help the early childhood educator to use Web-based units, this "safari" is a trip you'll want to plan with your class. Featured with the pages is a Teacher's Guide with a list of related print titles. To round out this unit, there are some great companion worksheets at the abcteach Web site.

Evaluation:

Students will begin a study of insect life cycles with a connection to literature.

Resources:

Schoolyard Science: Ladybugs
      <http://www.geocities.com/sseagraves/schoolyardscience.htm>
abcteach: Ladybugs
      <http://www.abcteach.com/Themeunits/Ladybugs/LadybugTOC.htm>

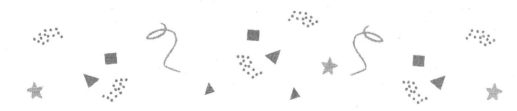

Celebrate Remember the Alamo Day

Subject: Social Studies

Grade level: 4 to 5

> Celebrate the famous battle at the Alamo (March 6, 1836) when the Mexican General Santa Ana defeated the Texans

Activity Title:
Texan Heroes

Materials:

Whiteboard, student journals, Web site access

Procedure:

Use the whiteboard to define heroism. Ask the students to list several heroes in history. Use the Web or print resources to research this famous battle. To what does the cry "Remember the Alamo!" refer? Who was David Crockett?

Evaluation:

Students will study heroism by learning about this famous battle in American history.

Resources:

Garland, Sherry. *A Line in the Sand: The Alamo Diary of Lucinda Lawrence, Gonzales, Texas 1835.*
    New York: Scholastic, 1995.
The Alamo
    <http://www.thealamo.org>
Remember the Alamo!
    <http://www.kwanah.com/txmilmus/tnghist3.htm>

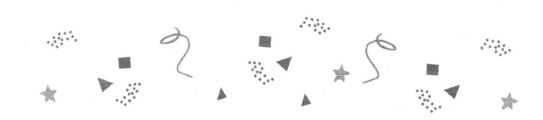

Activity 22:

Celebrate National Women's History Month

Subject: Social Studies

Grade level: 4 to 5

In March, learn about the achievements women have made by celebrating National Women's History Month. Celebrate March 8, which is International Women's History Day.

Activity Title:
Neighborhood Women

Materials:

Whiteboard, student journal, class visit

Procedure:

Use the whiteboard with your students to brainstorm names of famous women in history. Ask the students to tell what contributions they have made to history.

Research local women's organizations to find a volunteer to come to the classroom to discuss her struggle with equality. Expect some resistance by students to be able to recognize this topic as valid.

Take this opportunity to add this topic to your list of lessons in reflective journaling.

Evaluation:

Students will focus on learning about women who have contributed to science, history, the arts, and society through the ages.

Resources:

ALFY's Women in History Theme
<http://www.alfy.com/teachers/teach/thematic_units/Women_In_History/WH_1.asp>
Women in American History
<http://women.eb.com/>

Celebrate Telephone Patent Day

Subject: Social Studies, Reading

Grade level: 5

Celebrate the day the telephone received its patent on March 7, 1876.

Activity Title:
Hello?

Materials:

Web site access, books on the topic, newspaper and magazine articles on the use of cellular phones while driving, student journals

Procedure:

The telephone has changed how we communicate. Nothing demands more attention than the ring of the telephone! Research the invention of the telephone by using print and Web resources.

Use the student journals to have the students write about their readings including the current controversy over the use of the cellular phone while driving. Have your students ever seen a dial telephone? Does your classroom even have a telephone?

Evaluation:

Students will explore the beginnings of the use of the telephone and apply that to modern cellular telephone issues.

Resources:

Patent for the Telephone
    <http://www.nara.gov/education/cc/edbell.html>
The Alexander Graham Bell Family Papers
    <http://memory.loc.gov/ammem/bellhtml/belhome.html>

Celebrate National Peanut Month

Subject: Social Studies

Grade level: 5

Celebrate the life of George Washington Carver, a great inventor who did much more than invent the peanut.

Activity Title:
Just Peanuts?

Materials:

Encyclopedia (traditional print, CD-ROM, or Web-based), student journals, books on peanut farming and the inventor

Procedure:

Have the students investigate and prepare a report on the life of "The Peanut Man."

Have them consider how many products are made from peanuts, where they grow, and if anyone in the class or school is allergic to them.

Evaluation:

Students will study the life of an American educator and inventor.

Resources:

Carter, Andy. *George Washington Carver*. Minneapolis: Carolrhoda Books, 2001.
Inventor George Washington Carver
    <http:// www.ideafinder.com/history/inventors/carver.htm>

Celebrate the Ides of March

Subject: Interdisciplinary

Grade level: 5

Beware the Ides of March! On March 15, 44 BC, Julius Caesar ignored a warning and was stabbed to death.

Activity Title:
Dangerous Warnings

Materials:
Whiteboard, student journals

Procedure:
Relate the story of Julius Caesar to the class. Explain that he was warned about dangers and ignored them, and this slogan has endured to this day. Take this opportunity to talk to the class about personal safety at school, outside, at home, and when using the Internet.

Students can write safety tips in their journals.

Evaluation:
Students will learn about personal safety.

Resources:
National Safety Council
    <http://www.nsc.org/library/facts.htm>
CyberCitizen
    <http://www.cybercitizenship.org/>

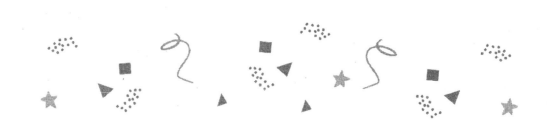

Celebrate National Quilting Day

Subject: Reading, Social Studies, Art

Grade level: 5

Celebrate March 17 as National Quilting Day as part of a study of the Underground Railroad.

Activity Title:
Communicate with Quilts

Materials:

Large square graph paper, Web site access, art materials

Procedure:

Start a discussion of oral history by connecting the art of quilting with the study of the Underground Railroad. It is said that quilt patterns were used as communication signals to help the slaves on their way to freedom. Is this truth or folktale?

Learn about quilting with the help of the art teacher.

Evaluation:

Students will learn how the Underground Railroad communicated using quilts.

Resources:

Hopkinson, Deborah. *Sweet Clara and the Freedom Quilt.* New York: Knopf, 1996.
Underground Railroad Quilts
    <http://www.beavton.k12.or.us/Greenway/leahy/ugrr/quilts.htm>
The World Wide Quilting Page Coloring Book
    <http://ttsw.com/ColoringBook/QuiltColoringBook.html>

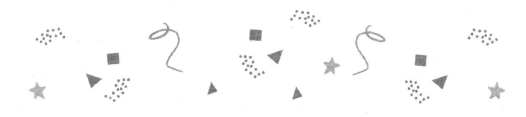

Activity 27:

Celebrate St. Patrick's Day

Subject: Interdisciplinary

Grade level: K to 5

Celebrate St. Patrick's Day on March 17 with the wearing o' the green.

Activity Title:
Potato Prints

Materials:

Suggested readings and Web sites on potato printing to find the needed materials for the activity

Procedure:

Start the day with a reading of an Irish folktale. Students of all grades will enjoy an art project of making vegetable prints. Your students probably will wind up wearing the green paint, so be prepared!

As a journal activity, have the students record the steps they took to create their print.

Evaluation:

Students will explore Irish folktales and create potato print artwork.

Resources:

DePaola, Tomie. *Jamie O'Rourke and the Big Potato*. New York: G.P. Putnam and Sons, 1992.
Haddad, Helen R. *Potato Printing*. New York: Thomas Y. Crowell, 1981.
Pomeroy, Diana. *One Potato: A Counting Book of Potato Prints*. San Diego: Harcourt, Brace and Co., 1996.
Home and Garden Potato Printing Project
   <http://www.hgtv.com/HGTV/project/0,1158,FOLI_project_15383,FF.html>
Potato Stamps
   <http://wolfen.wolfe.k12.ky.us/globe/spuds/POSTAM.HTM>
Rainbow Paper Plate Activity
   <http://www.enchantedlearning.com/crafts/stpatrick/rainbowstreamer/>

Celebrate Tessellation Day

Subject: Art, Math

Grade level: 5

Explore the world of Escher by learning about repeating patterns called tessellations.

Activity Title:
Repeat That Again

Materials:

Student journals, pattern blocks, paper and art supplies

Procedure:

Continue your classroom exploration of patterns by learning about Escher's art and the math of tessellations. Create paper tessellations with the help of the art teacher. Remember, tessellations must have no gaps or spaces in the pattern as it covers the work area.

Evaluation:

Students will continue to study repeating patterns in a combined art and math unit.

Resources:

(Related Activity) Escher, M.C. *The M.C. Escher Coloring Book: 24 Images to Color.* New York: Harry N. Abrams, 1995.
Tessellation Tutorials
<http://forum.swarthmore.edu/sum95/suzanne/tess.intro.html>

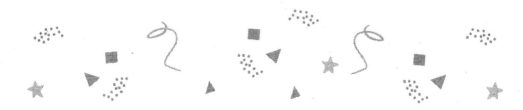

Activity 29:
Celebrate Kite Day

Subject: Interdisciplinary
Grade level: 4 to 5

With March's windy nature, it is the perfect time to spend rainy days making kites and sunny, windy days flying them. What better way to welcome spring?

Activity Title:
Go Fly a Kite!

Materials:
Web site access, books on the topic, art materials

Procedure:
The Web is flying high with kite resources that connect strongly to curriculum topics. This whole-class project can result in one kite, a kite for each small group, or mini individual kites.

If you have older students in your school, this is a wonderful collaborative project among grade levels.

Evaluation:
Students will learn the history of kite flying, and practice creating and flying kites.

Resources:
Famous Kite Flights
     <http://www.total.net/~kite/famous.html>
The Virtual Kite Zoo: Kites in the Classroom
     <http://www.kites.org/zoo/class.html>
Lesson Plan: Soar into Spring with Kites!
     <http://www.education-world.com/a_lesson/lesson056.shtml>

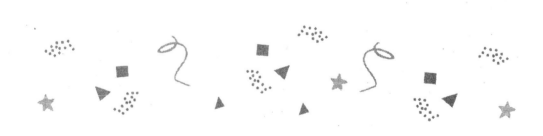

Celebrate Spring!

Subject: Science
Grade level: 3 to 5

On March 20 or 21, spring arrives! Even if it doesn't feel or look like spring outside your classroom, this is a good day to celebrate learning about the vernal equinox.

Activity Title:
Equal Time

Materials:

Web site access, whiteboard, calendar, model or chart of the Sun and Earth, raw eggs, science books or encyclopedias (traditional paper, CD-ROM, or Web-based)

Procedure:

Begin the study of spring by teaching about the equinox.

If you want to try the suggested egg-related science experiment, you may want to have some parents come in to help out.

Evaluation:

Students will understand the concept of the vernal equinox.

Resources:

Gibbons, Gail. *The Reason for Seasons*. New York: Holiday House, 1995.
The Vernal Equinox
      <http://www.teachervision.com/lesson-plans/lesson-5486.html>
Eggs and the Vernal Equinox
      <http://web.physics.twsu.edu/facsme/vernale.htm>

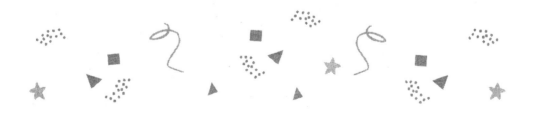

Celebrate Spring Holidays

Subject: Interdisciplinary
Grade level: K to 5

Celebrate the arrival of spring by learning about the holidays celebrated during this time. If this is not part of your curriculum, take today to learn about Daylight Savings Time.

Activity Title:
Spring Ahead!

Materials:
Web site access, books on the topic

Procedure:
Breathe a sigh of relief, open the classroom windows, and experience the wonder of spring. Teachers can find a lot of ideas for spring holiday lessons from the Kids Domain Web site plus teach a lesson on daylight saving time.

Explore the meaning of the saying "Spring ahead, fall back" with the students.

Evaluation:
Students will learn about spring holidays and understand how daylight saving time works.

Resources:
Kids Domain: Easter
    <http://www.kidsdomain.com/holiday/easter/index.html>
Kids Domain: Passover
    <http://www.kidsdomain.com/holiday/passover/index.html>
Daylight Saving Time
    <http://webexhibits.org/daylightsaving/index.html>

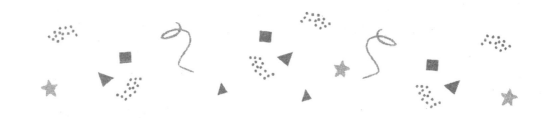

Celebrate Harry Houdini's Birthday

Subject: Interdisciplinary

Grade level: 4 to 5

Celebrate the Birthday (March 24) of Harry Houdini by learning about the world's most famous magician.

Activity Title:

Magic Secrets

Materials:

Whiteboard, books on the subject

Procedure:

Houdini was often described as "larger than life," though he was only 5 feet, 6 inches tall. Ask your students what they think that means and to think of someone in today's world who might be described in that way. As you have the students learn about Houdini's life, ask them if some of his tricks were too dangerous.

Invite a local magician to perform sleight of hand tricks.

Evaluation:

Students will learn about a famous performer and what risks he took with his life.

Resources:

Kulling, Marcia. *The Great Houdini*. New York: Random House, 1999.
Borland, Kathryn Kilby. *Harry Houdini: Young Magician*. New York: Macmillan, 1991.
The American Experience: Houdini
    <http://www.pbs.org/wgbh/amex/houdini/>

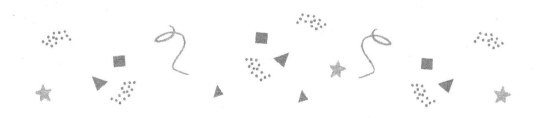

Celebrate National Nutrition Month

Subject: Health

Grade level: 2 to 4

Celebrate March as National Nutrition Month with a study of the five food groups.

Activity Title:
Food Pyramid

Materials:

Web site access, food magazines, whiteboard, art supplies

Procedure:

Continue learning about healthy food habits with an exploration of which foods should be consumed daily. Create a classroom collage of healthy foods and see if they are on the school lunch menu.

Students can begin a food diary in their journal, which can easily become a home-school connection project.

Evaluation:

Students will learn about the five food groups.

Resources:

Food Guide Pyramid
    <http://www.nal.usda.gov:8001/py/pmap.htm>
Nutrition Explorations: Food Groups
    <http://www.nutritionexplorations.org/teacher_central/fabfood.html>

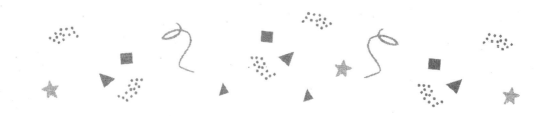

Celebrate Robert Frost's Birthday

Subject: Reading

Grade level: 3 to 5

> The American poet Robert Frost was born on March 26, 1874. Celebrate his birthday by learning about poetry.

Activity Title:

Poetry

Materials:

Poetry books, student journals, Web site access

Procedure:

Every classroom teacher has a favorite poetry lesson. Use Robert Frost's birthday to read and write poetry.

Evaluation:

Students will begin a spring poetry unit by reading about Robert Frost.

Resources:

Schmidt, Gary D. (ed.). *Poetry for Young People: Robert Frost.* New York: Sterling, 1994.
Frost, Robert. *You Come Too. Favorite Poems for Young People.* New York: Henry Holt, 1987.
Giggle Poetry
    <http://www.gigglepoetry.com>
How to Write Funny Poems
    <http://www.poetryteachers.com/poetclass/poetclass.html>

Activity 34:

Celebrate Egg Incubator Invention Day

Subject: Science

Grade level: K to 5

> Bridge your way from March to April by teaching about raising chicks on the day the egg incubator was invented (March 30).

Activity Title:
Chicken or Egg?

Materials:

Web site access, materials for raising chicks

Procedure:

Use Susan Seagrave's "eggscellent" classroom Web resource on raising chicks. She has listed books, projects, experiments, and instructions for the project.

Older students can use the Chickscope project to build their own incubator and to learn more on embryology via the Web. It's something to "eggsperience"!

Evaluation:

Students will study embryology as a spring science unit.

Resources:

Chickscope Project
   <http://chickscope.beckman.uiuc.edu>
From Egg to Chick
   <http://www.geocities.com/sseagraves/fromeggtochick.htm>

Celebrate Pencil Invention Day

Subject: Reading, Writing

Grade level: 1 to 4

Celebrate the invention of the pencil with the attached eraser on March 30th, 1858, by Hyman Lipman.

Activity Title:
Sharp Point

Materials:
Pencils, student journals

Procedure:
Have the students examine a pencil and describe its characteristics.

Use the library or the Web to research the invention of the pencil. Ask the students to "invent" a new pencil and write about it in their student journals. Illustrations should be done in pencil, of course!

Evaluation:
Students will investigate the history of the commonest of classroom tools-the pencil.

Resources:
Foreman, Michael. *Grandfather's Pencil and the Room of Stories*. San Diego, CA: Harcourt Brace, 1994.
The Pencil Pages
    <http://www.pencil.com>

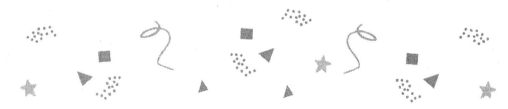

❖ April ❖

Activity 36:

Celebrate April Fool's Day

Subject: Language Arts

Grade level: 3 to 5

Celebrate April 1 with a smile and an emphasis on appropriate use of humor.

Activity Title:
Foolish Fools

Materials:

Whiteboard, student journals

Procedure:

Use the whiteboard to brainstorm the possible reasons for this holiday. Explain to the students the calendar we use today was not always the same. New Year's Day was celebrated on different days and different months of the year. When the first day of January was decreed as the first day of the New Year (in 1562), people made fun of those who didn't switch to celebrate the holiday on that day, calling them April Fools. They sent out false party invitations to trick them.

Have the students reflect in their journals about a time they may have been tricked or misled.

Evaluation:

Students will learn about the traditions of this holiday and talk about feelings.

Resources:

April Fool's Day
  <http://www.umkc.edu/imc/aprilfoo.htm>
Franklin Institute: Tricked by the Calendar
  <http://www/fi.edu/qa99/spotlight4/index.html>

Celebrate National Laugh Week

Subject: Writing and Presentation Skills

Grade level: 4 to 5

The first week of April has everyone laughing out loud. Laughter promotes good health in us all.

Activity Title:
Laugh Out Loud

Materials:
Student journals, Web site access

Procedure:
Telling a joke is a good way to begin teaching simple presentation skills. Have the students write their favorite joke or funny story in their student journal.

After editing the jokes, have one student present their joke to the class each day of this month.

Evaluation:
Students will learn simple presentation skills by writing a favorite joke and then presenting it to the class.

Resources:
April Fool's Day
    <http://www.usis.usemb.se/Holidays/celebrate/april.html>
Billy Bear's Jokes for Kids
    <http://www.billybear4kids.com/show/jokes.htm>
abcteach: Joke/Riddle Book Report Form
    <http://www.abcteach.com/bookreports/jokeriddle.htm>

Celebrate National Library Week

Subject: Reading

Grade level: 1 to 5

Celebrate National Library Week with a visit to the public library. This is a good time to prepare for the Turn Off TV Week by introducing your class to the variety of materials available at the public library

Activity Title:

Library Visit

Materials:

Trip to the library, Web site access

Procedure:

Have your students take a tour of the public library in your city or town. Some students may never have visited the adult room, met the Library Director, or learned about the library programs. The library may have some special events planned for this week in which students may participate.

Evaluation:

Students will learn about the variety of services available at the public library.

Resources:

National Library Week
    <http://www.ala.org/pio/nlw>

Celebrate Learning About Fractals

Subject: Math

Grade level: 5

April is National Mathematics Month, so celebrate by learning about the world of chaos.

Activity Title:
Math Art

Materials:

Web site access, color inkjet printer and paper

Procedure:

Even if the math concepts presented are too difficult for your entire class, all students will enjoy viewing and printing fractal art. Although there are many fractal-generating computer software applications, they may be too computer-intensive if you have an older classroom computer. They are so beautiful that it's hard to believe they are mathematically generated!

Evaluation:

Students will begin to study higher-level mathematical concepts with an introduction to fractals.

Resources:

Cynthia Lanius's Lessons in Fractals
    <http://math.rice.edu/~lanius/frac/>
Fractal Art by Wizzle
    <http://www.mathemagicimages.com/fractals/fractalintro.htm>
42Explore Topic: Fractals
    <http://eduscapes.com/42explore/fractal.htm>

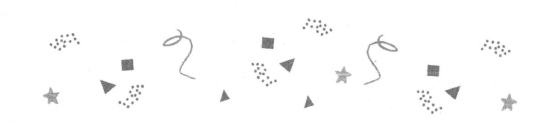

Celebrate National Siblings Day

Subject: Interdisciplinary

Grade level: 4 to 5

National Siblings Day is held to honor all brothers and sisters. Set aside April 10 to teach a special journal activity on the pros and cons of having siblings.

Activity Title:

Siblings

Materials:

Whiteboard, student journals, dictionaries (traditional paper, CD-ROM, or Web-based)

Procedure:

Use the whiteboard to ask the students to define the word "sibling" without looking it up.

Have students use a dictionary and see how accurately the definition matched the one defined by guessing.

Make a class list of siblings. Who has the most, the fewest, none, is adopted?

Have the students reflect in their journal about siblings.

Evaluation:

Students will complete a reflective journal activity on siblings.

Resources:

National Siblings Day
<http://www.siblings-day.com>

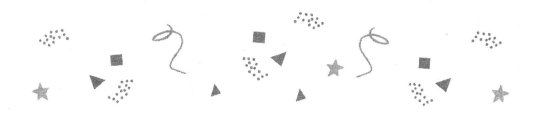

Celebrate National Turn Off TV Week

Subject: Interdisciplinary

Grade level: 4 to 5

> Turn off the television for seven days at school and at home, and celebrate the renewed connection of spending more time with family and friends. Celebrate this event during the third week in April.

Activity Title:
Commercial Free

Materials:

Books for reading for pleasure, outdoor activities, home dinner table parties

Procedure:

Brainstorm with your students to develop activities that can be enjoyed with family and friends for seven television-free days. Check with local businesses to see if they are sponsoring special events. Teachers should turn off the TV, too!

Have students investigate who invented TV and what TV was like in the "olden days."

Evaluation:

Students will participate in a week with no television and see what life was like before TV was invented.

Resources:

TV Land
    <http://www.tvland.com>
Inventing Television
    <http://www.inventorsmuseum.com/television.htm>

Celebrate Paul Revere's Ride Day

Subject: Social Studies

Grade level: 4 to 5

> On April 19, Massachusetts celebrates Patriot's Day to honor American patriots like Paul Revere. Even if you don't celebrate this day in your state, take time to learn about this important date in history.

Activity Title:
One if by Land

Materials:
Printed copy of Henry Wadsworth Longfellow's 1860 poem, Web site access

Procedure:
To demonstrate how history can come alive in a poem, read Longfellow's poem to the whole class. If you have Web site access, you can obtain a copy at the Paul Revere House. Don't miss the many activities available at this Web site for your students.

Evaluation:
Students will learn about the famous ride of Paul Revere.

Resources:
The Paul Revere House: The Midnight Ride
    <http://www.paulreverehouse.org/midnight.html>
The Paul Revere House: Just for Kids
    <http://www.paulreverehouse.org/justforkids/activities.html>

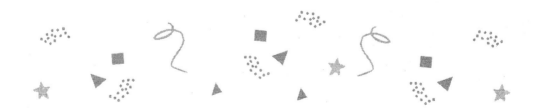

Celebrate Kindergarten Day

Subject: Interdisciplinary

Grade level: K to 5

Celebrate Kindergarten Day in your school with an interactive event just for that grade.

Activity Title:
Kindergarten Visit

Materials:

Procedure:

In many schools, the kindergarten students are separated from the rest of the school. Bring them into your classroom to see "what the big kids" do all day. Have your students plan this event. What do they think kindergarten students will want to know about their classroom? What memories do they have of that grade?

Have your students visit the kindergarten classroom and write in their student journals reflections on their physical and mental growth since they were kindergartners.

The Web sites for teachers of kindergarten students are growing as teachers share successful practices on the Internet. These Web sites are full of thematic ideas to be shared with other teachers of the early primary grades.

Evaluation:

Students will revisit the beginning of their school experience by planning for a visit to their classroom by the youngest members of the school.

Resources:

Mrs. Fischer's Kindergarten Themes
    <http://www.geocities.com/teachermom22/>
Kathy Schrock's Guide for Educators: Early Childhood Education Sites
    <http://school.discovery.com/schrockguide/edres.html#ece>

Activity 44:

Celebrate National Poetry Month

Subject: Reading, Writing

Grade level: 3 to 5

Celebrate National Poetry Month with the reading of poetry and the analysis of mood and color in poems.

Activity Title:
The Moods and Colors of Poetry by Gayle Bradbury

Materials:

Suggested readings; sheets of construction paper in red, blue, and yellow; pictures of faces cut from magazines that illustrate expressions of anger, happiness and sadness; whiteboard, student journals

Procedure:

Visualize the Color (Use *Hailstones and Halibut Bones: Adventures in Color.*)

This activity uses "What is Red?" "What is Blue?" "What is Yellow?"

Cut the construction paper into squares. Cut pictures of faces from magazines.

Explain the relationship between moods and colors by using the color blue as an example. Read aloud the poem about the color blue. How does blue make us feel? Brainstorm words and phrases like "sad," "feeling low," and "depressed." Repeat the same exercise for red and yellow. You can have students write some of these words in their student journals.

Ask the students how the three poems are alike. Distribute a square of each color of construction paper to each student. Which colors represent which moods?

Hold up a picture to the entire class of a face that shows emotion. Ask the students to match which emotion the picture expresses to a color. Distribute the rest of the pictures randomly and ask the students to match a picture to a color.

Listen for the Mood (Use *Me Is How I Feel: Poems.*)

Read "Wiggly Giggles" aloud to the class and have the students pick the color that matches the mood of the poem. Use the whiteboard to have the students brainstorm which words gave the clues to the mood of the poem.

Repeat this exercise with the readings of "And I Just Got Blamed Again" and "Disappointed."

Extension Activities

Create a class collage of each color, adding pictures, words, and other poems on large pieces of construction paper. Do one color per week and display the collages in the classroom.

Have the students create mini-collages in their student journals.

Evaluation:

Students will learn to appreciate how poetry can demonstrate sensitivity in moods and feelings and how colors can represent a wide range of emotions.

Resources:

Crossen, Stacy Jo, and Natalie Ann Covell. *Me Is How I Feel: Poems*. New York: McCall Publishing, 1970.

O'Neill, Mary LeDuc. *Hailstones and Halibut Bones: Adventures in Color*. New York: Doubleday, 1989.
   TeacherView: Hailstones and Halibut Bones
   <http://www.eduplace.com/tview/hailstonesandhalibutbones.html>

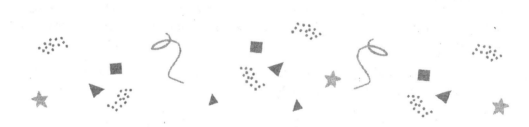

Celebrate National Playground Safety Week

Subject: Art, Character Education
Grade level: 4 to 5

Celebrate being safe and having fun before and after school during this third week of April.

Activity Title:
Smart Play

Materials:

Whiteboard, school playground rules, town playground location and rules, art supplies

Procedure:

Use the whiteboard to record what the students know about the rules for the school playground. Be sure to include the school district policy for strangers on school property.

Have the students design posters to hang in the school cafeteria reflecting the rules of playgrounds.

Evaluation:

Students will review safe play on playgrounds.

Resources:

National Program for Playground Safety
<http://www.uni.edu/playground/home.html>

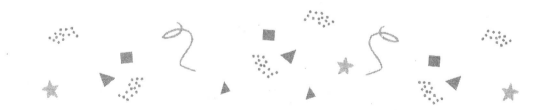

Activity 46:
Celebrate Earth Day

Subject: Science, Language Arts
Grade level: 1 to 5

Awareness of the need for respect for our planet doesn't have to wait to be introduced until the middle or high school environmental science class. Celebrate Earth Day on or around April 22 with some ideas designed especially for young students.

Activity Title:
Taking Care of Earth

Materials:
Web site access

Procedure:
Sandy Kemsley's Web site (abcteach) has some great ideas for celebrating this day in the classroom. By visiting her resource page, you can print out ready-to-use ideas for the elementary classroom. Have your student perform an Earth Day rap, take part in a group activity, do crossword puzzles and word searches, and perform research. These great ideas deserve applause!

Evaluation:
Students will investigate important environmental issues.

Resources:
abcteach: Earth Day Resources
    <http://abcteach.com/earthday/earthtoc.htm>

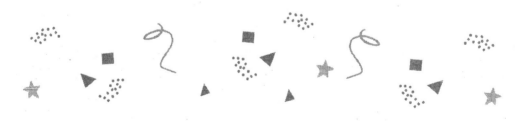

Celebrate Oral History Day

Subject: Social Studies

Grade level: 5

Celebrate April 26 as Oral History Day by teaching a lesson on the growing importance of recording past historical events.

Activity Title:

Remembered History

Materials:

Web site access, tape recorders, whiteboard, student journals, word processing application

Procedure:

For those people who could not write, oral history has been one way to pass on important stories, memories, and events from one generation to another. Some cultures have used pictorial methods to accomplish this recording of history. The disadvantage of recording history orally is that the accuracy of the recording and of the interpretation of the recording may be questionable.

Students may have learned about oral history as they listened to family stories and looked at family photographs. Ask the students if family members agree on what actually happened at a past family gathering. Journal writing is an excellent method of recording oral history.

Investigate the suggested Web site for ideas on how to use oral history with your curriculum.

Evaluation:

Students will learn about the benefits and disadvantages of oral history.

Resources:

Lawlor, Veronica. *I Was Dreaming to Come to America: Memories from the Ellis Island Oral History Project*. New York: Viking, 1995.
42Explore Topic: Oral History
    <http://eduscapes.com/42explore/oralhst.htm>

Celebrate John Audubon's Birthday

Subject: Science, Language Arts

Grade level: 3 to 4

April 26 is for the birds! Celebrate the life of naturalist John Audubon by learning about your state bird.

Activity Title:
Fine Feathered Friends

Materials:

Field guides to bird watching, Web site access, student journals

Procedure:

Have the students use the school library, a field guide, or the Audubon Web site to find out your state's official bird.

Research this bird by using field guides. The Peterson Field Guides for Young Naturalists are useful reading for both students and their teachers.

Evaluation:

Students will learn more about their state bird.

Resources:

Audubon Society: List of State Birds
   <http://www.audubon.org/statebirds/index.html>

Activity 49:

Celebrate Arbor Day

Subject: Science
Grade level: K to 5

Celebrate Arbor Day on the last Friday of April. This holiday is celebrated internationally as a way to remind us of the necessity of taking care of our trees and forests.

Activity Title:
Shade of a Tree

Materials:

Web site access, books on the topic, trees to plant on school or community property

Procedure:

Schools often celebrate this day with the annual planting of a tree on school property. Some local nursery or garden organization may be happy to donate a tree or small bush for the school grounds.

Take this opportunity to extend the lessons from last fall on photosynthesis and ecology. Students can identify local trees, using their journals for recording the findings. Younger students can create shape books, collect leaves, and read tree poems.

Connect this to the following activity on learning about paper. Some students may not know paper is made from trees.

Evaluation:

Students will learn about the planting and care of our trees and forests.

Resources:

42Explore Topic: Trees and Forests
    <http://eduscapes.com/42explore/treesforests.htm>
abcteach: Trees Theme Unit
    <http://www.abcteach.com/trees/treestoc.htm>

Celebrate Paper Making Day

Subject: Art

Grade level: 4 to 5

Celebrate paper making day by learning about the different kinds of paper and how paper is manufactured.

Activity Title:
Recycle Paper

Materials:

Web site access, samples of different kinds of paper, student journals

Procedure:

Making your own paper is a fun, but messy, project. Use the Web to find out how paper is made by hand and by modern manufacturing methods.

Have students gather scraps of different types of paper to create a paper collage.

Have them investigate what a watermark is and why high quality paper has them.

Evaluation:

Students will see the relationship between our forests and the making of paper.

Resources:

42Explore Topic: Paper Making
    <http://eduscapes.com/42explore/papermaking.htm>

Activity 51:

Celebrate May Day

Subject: Interdisciplinary

Grade level: 5

Celebrate May Day with a traditional May breakfast for the teachers and staff.

Activity Title:

May Day

Materials:

May breakfast buffet (food and decorations provided by the parents), flyer invitation materials, class schedule of duties for students

Procedure:

Have students plan a simple May breakfast buffet for the teachers and staff. Enlist the help of parents to provide the funds or supplies for the decorations and food. Students can plan the event, create a flyer for the teachers, set up the table in the school cafeteria, serve the food, and clean up. This is a great teacher appreciation event and ties into National Egg Month, too!

Evaluation:

Students will participate in planning an event to be held at their school.

Resources:

'Round the Maypole: Celebrating May Day
<http://www.umkc.edu/imc/mayday.htm>

Celebrate National Wildflower Week

Subject: Interdisciplinary

Grade level: 2 to 3

National Wildflower Week is dedicated to the appreciation of native wildflowers.

Activity Title:

Wild About Flowers

Materials:

Web site access, books about wildflowers

Procedure:

Have students brainstorm wildflowers they see in their neighborhood.

As a class project, have the students research the state flower. Use the suggested Web sites to view the wildflowers for each state on a stamp.

Evaluation:

Students will investigate wildflowers found in their state and learn more about their state wildflower.

Resources:

State Flowers
    <http://www.50states.com/flower.htm>
State Flowers on Stamps
    <http://pss.uvm.edu/ppp/statefls.htm>

Activity 53:

Celebrate National Egg Month

Subject: Interdisciplinary

Grade level: 2 to 4

Celebrate May as National Egg Month with some egg-citing activities in the classroom.

Activity Title:
Egg-citement

Materials:

Web site access, supplies for the Egg Drop Day

Procedure:

Eggs can make a great interdisciplinary learning unit with a main focus on science. Visit the Web to learn about the "Egg Day Drop" that one school holds every year on Egg Day. All the materials you will need to have an event like this in your school are listed there.

Younger children have their own Egg WebQuest to use for this day.

Evaluation:

Students will explore an interdisciplinary theme of eggs. It's "egg-citing" to learn about eggs!

Resources:

Egg Fun
    <http://www.eecs.umich.edu/mathscience/funexperiments/agesubject/lessons/egg2.html>
Egg Day Drop
    <http://deafed.educ.kent.edu/970218b.htm>
Are Chickens the Only Ones? WebQuest for Grade 1
    <http://warrensburg.k12.mo.us/webquest/animals/index.htm>

Activity 54:

Celebrate American Bike Month

Subject: Interdisciplinary
Grade level: K to 5

Celebrate National Bike Safety Month with activities on bike safety.

Activity Title:
Bike Safety

Materials:
Web site access

Procedure:
This month is a great time for students to get out after school and ride their bikes. Invite the local police department to come to the school to talk about bike safety and the rules of the road for bicycles.

Use the suggested Web site for some classroom ideas.

Evaluation:
Bicycle safety tips will be reinforced for students.

Resources:
Creative Classroom Bike Safety Lesson Plans
    <http://www.creativeclassroom.org/subaru/lesson-plans.html>

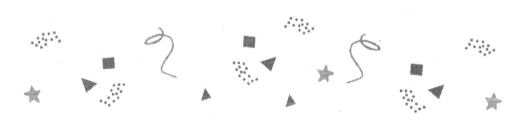

Celebrate Cinco de Mayo

Subject: Interdisciplinary

Grade level: 4 to 5

May 5 is the celebration of the Mexican victory at the Battle of Puebla in 1862. Many Mexican Americans consider this a modern cultural celebration.

Activity Title:

Fiesta!

Materials:

Web site access, traditional Mexican food for the fiesta

Procedure:

Lift your classroom's spirits with a study of this popular cultural holiday. Combine a fiesta with a mini-study of Spanish. Have the students plan a classroom fiesta with a piñata and snacks of Mexican food. Ask for parent volunteers. Play traditional Mexican music. Ole!

Evaluation:

Students will plan a classroom fiesta.

Resources:

Menard, Valerie. *The Latino Holiday Book: From Cinco de Mayo to Dia de los Muertos-the Celebrations and Traditions of Hispanic-Americans.* New York: Marlowe and Co., 2000.
Cinco de Mayo (for teachers)
    <http://www.umkc.edu/imc/cincomay.htm>
NOBLE Cinco de Mayo Web Resources
    <http://www.noblenet.org/year/tty5cin.htm>

Celebrate Leo Lionni's Birthday

Subject: Reading

Grade level: 2 to 4

Continue the celebration of National Egg Month with a reading of Leo Lionni's book on or around his birthday of May 5.

Activity Title:

Extraordinary

Materials:

Suggested book by the author

Procedure:

Have students use dictionary and thesaurus skills (traditional print, CD-ROM, or Web-based) to define "extraordinary," writing this definition and various synonyms in their journals.

Have the students write about an extraordinary event that has occurred in their lives during this school year. Ask them to reflect if it is okay to be just ordinary.

Read the suggested book to the class.

Evaluation:

Students will be introduced to an author by the reading of the author's book on his birthday.

Resources:

Lionni, Leo. *An Extraordinary Egg*. New York: Knopf, 1994.
The Extraordinary Egg Resources
<http://www.canadaegg.ca/english/educat/educat.html>

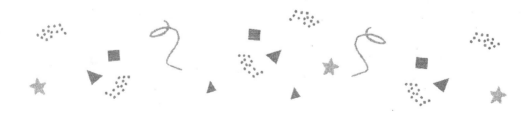

Celebrate Peter Pan Day

Subject: Reading, Science

Grade level: 2 to 4

> May 9 is the birthday of Sir James M. Barrie, whose delightful story of Peter Pan is well known.

Activity Title:
Never Grow Up

Materials:
Web site access, suggested reading, large paper and pencils, bright light

Procedure:
Visit the Web or the school or public library to locate a copy of Peter Pan. In chapter two, Peter leaves behind his shadow. In chapter three, he returns looking for it. Ask the students what they know about shadows. Can they be sewed back on? Was this an ordinary shadow?

Use the Web to learn more about shadows.

Have the students create a shadow outline of an ordinary object or a shadow outline of their profile as an end-of-the year gift for their parents or guardians.

Evaluation:
Students will investigate shadows.

Resources:
Peter Pan: Chapter 3: "Come Away, Come Away"
    <http://www.hoboes.com/html/FireBlade/Barrie/Peter/chapter3.html>
What Are Shadows?
    <http://www.geocities.com/Heartland/7134/Shadow/ghshadows.htm>
The Shadow Quiz
    <http://www.geocities.com/Heartland/7134/Shadow/ghquiz2.htm>

Celebrate National Strawberry Month

Subject: Science, Art, Math

Grade level: 3 to 5

Celebrate the sweetness of this month by learning about strawberries.

Activity Title:

Strawberry Sweet

Materials:

Whole strawberries, encyclopedias (traditional print, CD-ROM, or Web-based)

Procedure:

Before starting this project, poll the class to make sure no student is allergic to strawberries.

As a journal art project, have the students draw strawberries, both whole and cut in half. The classroom will smell delicious! Combine this activity with tomorrow's tea party!

Use the encyclopedia to research strawberries. Create a list of popular fruits of your students and graph the results. Which one is the class favorite?

Evaluation:

Students will learn various qualities of strawberries.

Resources:

Strawberries: A to Z Science Discovery Channel School
    <http://school.discovery.com/homeworkhelp/worldbook/atozscience/s/535960.html>
Jamming with Strawberries
    <http://www.umkc.edu/imc/strawber.htm>

Celebrate Tea Party Day

Subject: Science, Social Studies

Grade level: 3 to 5

Several cultures have important ceremonies at which tea is served. Celebrate this day (May 10), which is Sir Thomas Lipton's birthday, by learning about how tea is grown.

Activity Title:
Tea for Two

Materials:
Encyclopedias (print, CD-ROM, or Web-based), student journals, decaffeinated tea or iced tea to drink

Procedure:
Combine this activity with Activity 58 and have the students research strawberries and tea at the same time.

Have a classroom tea party!

Learn more about the Boston Tea Party. Was it really a party?

Evaluation:
Students will learn how and where tea is grown, and which countries use tea as part of a cultural ceremony

Resources:
A to Z Science: Tea
     <http://school.discovery.com/homeworkhelp/worldbook/atozscience/t/548900.html>
Famous Scots: Sir Thomas Lipton
     <http://www.tartans.com/articles/famscots/thomaslipton.html>

Celebrate Lobster Conservation Day

Subject: Reading, Science

Grade level: 2 to 5

Even young students can learn about the laws of conservation of nature. Take this month to learn about lobsters.

Activity Title:

Conserving Crustaceans

Materials:

Suggested reading, Web site access

Procedure:

Visit the public library to obtain a copy of the suggested book on lobsters or similar titles on lobster biology and the lobster industry. Visit the suggested Web sites to learn about an online project entitled Travel Buddies.

Use the Web to find out about lobsters. If possible, bring a live lobster to the classroom. Students can then relate what they learn to the live animal. Watch out for those claws!

Evaluation:

Students will investigate lobsters and the lobster industry.

Resources:

Ziefert, Harriet. *Bob and Shirley: A Tale of Two Lobsters*. New York: HarperCollins, 1991.
Lobster: Research Links for Students
    <http://www.stemnet.nf.ca/CITE/oceanlobsters.htm>
The Home of the Looneys: Travel Lobster Buddies
    <http://lee.boston.k12.ma.us/d4/trav/lroot.asp>

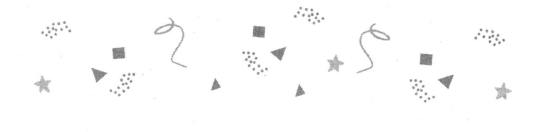

Celebrate National Teacher Appreciation Day

Subject: Writing
Grade level: 2 to 5

Appreciate the importance of teaching on National Teacher Day, which is celebrated on the first Tuesday in May.

Activity Title:
Thank a Teacher

Materials:

Writing materials, student journals

Procedure:

Have your students write a short letter of appreciation to another teacher or a former teacher in the building or district. This is a good time to remind students about the teacher specialists and those administrators that were (and still are) teachers.

As a journal activity, have students ask a parent to tell them a story about a teacher in the parent's past. The students can write about it in their journal. Have students reflect if teaching has changed since their parents' or grandparents' school days.

Evaluation:

Students will write a note of appreciation to a past teacher or staff member in the school district.

Resources:

Teacher Appreciation Day
    <http://www.nea.org/teachday/>

Celebrate Mother's Day

Subject: Art, Writing

Grade level: K to 2

Celebrate Mother's Day, which is the second Sunday in May, by learning to appreciate the hard work of a mother, stepmother, or grandmother.

Activity Title:

Coupons for Mom

Materials:

Art supplies, paper

Procedure:

Brainstorm with the class the ways they can be helpful at home. List the job responsibilities they have. Have them reflect upon which ones are most often forgotten.

Have students create a hand-drawn coupon to give to their mother, stepmother, or grandmother as a promise to help out with a specific task at home. Have students illustrate these coupons.

Evaluation:

Student will create a "coupon" to be redeemed by a busy mother.

Resources:

The Big Picture: Mother's Day
   <http://dailynews.yahoo.com/full_coverage/yahooligans/celebrate_moms>

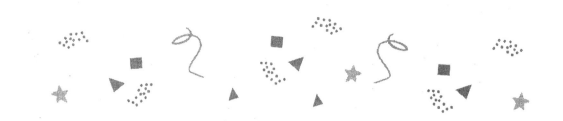

Celebrate Margret Rey's Birthday

Subject: Reading

Grade level: K to 3

Celebrate Margret Rey's birthday on May 16 in a "curious" way.

Activity Title:
Curious?

Materials:
Dictionary, thesaurus

Procedure:
Have the students use their dictionary skills to define "curious." How many synonyms can they find in a thesaurus for this word? Is anyone curious?

Read the suggested title or another title by this author that tie to your curriculum.

Use the suggested Web site to find an activity for your class.

Evaluation:
Students will learn about the rewards and consequences of being curious.

Resources:
Rey, Margret. *Curious George Flies a Kite*. Boston: Houghton Mifflin, 2000.
Curious George's Web Site Activities
    <http://www.curiousgeorge.com/travels/activities/index.html>

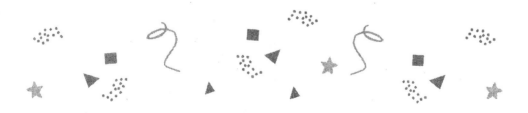

Celebrate Good Neighbor Day

Subject: Interdisciplinary

Grade level: 2 to 5

Celebrate the spirit of community on May 20, which is Good Neighbor Day.

Activity Title:
Neighbors

Materials:
Whiteboard, student journals

Procedure:

Use the whiteboard to have students brainstorm ideas of being a good neighbor. If the school is in a neighborhood, do the students know the neighbors adjacent to the building? If your students are seated at desks in your classroom, how can they be good neighbors to the others around them?

Have students write ideas about being good neighbors in their journals.

Connect this day to a unit on fairy tales and folktales with a reading of the suggested fable by Aesop.

Evaluation:
Students will brainstorm ways to be good neighbors in their school or community.

Resources:
Grasshopper and Owl: Neighbors Lesson by Aesop
 <http://www.teachervision.com/lesson-plans/lesson-4890.html>

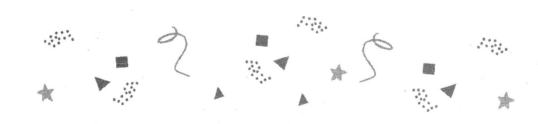

Celebrate Learning About Gardening

Subject: Science

Grade level: 4

Celebrate May's good weather by leaning about gardening. The experience of seed to plant as a science activity is beneficial to students for learning important skills in observation and measurement. Students may not have much experience with plants, so this is a good opportunity to start them with the background knowledge they will need for middle school science and math.

Activity Title:

Easy Gardens

Materials:

Web site access, field trip to a local garden, computer spreadsheet application, easy-to-grow plants and planting materials from a local garden club, digital camera, Reproducible Activity 2: KWL Graphic Organizer

Procedure:

Start this activity by deciding what plants are available to grow in the classroom in your region of the country. Ask the parent group to supply the materials from a town or city garden club. You may wish to purchase a few small starter plants for the measurement activity.

Plan time for students to research the plant chosen. What does the seed look like? Is it a flowering plant? How much light and water will it need? Will it be too cold or too hot to grow this plant in the classroom? Use Reproducible Activity 2: KWL Graphic Organizer to help students manage these questions.

Plan a field trip to a local garden for students to observe different types of plants and to take digital images of them to post in the classroom.

Start one plant from a seed even if it is a different plant from the ones you are growing to measure. This will give students experience with the concept of seed-to-plant. Create a class chart of jobs, with some students keeping track of the temperature, some recording the amount of light exposure, and so forth. Students should be assigned watering and measuring tasks.

Create a spreadsheet to record the measurement of plant growth from planting until the end of the school year.

Evaluation:

Students will learn about gardening with a hands-on activity.

Resources:

My First Garden
        <http://www.urbanext.uiuc.edu/firstgarden/>

Celebrate Student Diversity Day

Subject: Interdisciplinary

Grade level: K to 5

Use the power of the resources of the Web to learn more about student diversity. Students of all abilities share a classroom, and teachers need information to help all students learn best. Use this day to learn about technology and diverse needs.

Activity Title:
Think of Everyone

Materials:
Web site access

Procedure:
Use the Web to locate information to plan lessons and to find resources to help the parents of your students with special needs. Empower all learners in your classroom by knowing about current advances in computer technology.

Evaluation:
Students and teachers investigate how technology can help all students learn.

Resources:
Microsoft's Accessibility Web Pages
    <http://www.microsoft.com/enable/>
Apple's Disability Web Pages
    <http://www.apple.com/disability/>
CAST
    <http://www.cast.org>

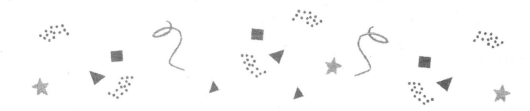

Celebrate Arnold Lobel's Birthday

Subject: Reading, Art

Grade level: 2 to 3

Celebrate Arnold Lobel's birthday on May 22 with a reading of his book Frog and Toad Are Friends.

Activity Title:
Pond Friends

Materials:

Suggested books by the author, Web site access, Venn diagram reproducible

Procedure:

Begin this activity with the author's book *Frog and Toad Are Friends*.

Use the Web to locate resources for the pond unit. As suggested by these Web sites, use Reproducible Activity 10: Venn Diagram Graphic Organizer to have the students list the qualities of Frog and Toad. How are they alike and different?

Extend this unit into the art curriculum to include the creation of an origami frog.

Evaluation:

Students will learn about friendship and begin a science unit on the pond.

Resources:

Lobel, Arnold. *Frog and Toad Are Friends*. New York: Harper & Row, 1970.
Frogs and Toads Are Friends but Still Different
    <http://www.teachers.net/lessons/posts/1027.html>
Cyberguide: Frog and Toad Are Friends
    <http://www.sdcoe.k12.ca.us/score/frog/frogtg.html>
Origami Jumping Frog
    <http://www.enchantedlearning.com/crafts/origami/frog/index.shtml>

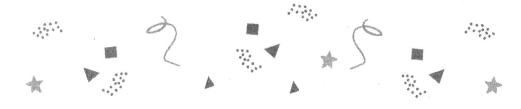

Celebrate National Geography Day

Subject: Geography

Grade level: 2 to 5

Celebrate National Geography Day on May 22 by learning about the continents.

Activity Title:

Continents

Materials:

Web site access, books on geography

Procedure:

Have the students begin a study of the continents. After making a list of the continents, divide the class into groups with each group representing a continent.

Use the various Web sites or books to have the group create a poster with some general facts about that continent.

Evaluation:

Students will select a continent of the world and begin a study of basic geography using maps.

Resources:

Outline Maps
    <http://www.eduplace.com/ss/ssmaps/index.html>
Geography at Enchanted Learning
    <http://www.enchantedlearning.com/geography/>
Knowing the Seven Continents
    <http://www.uwf.edu/coehelp/studentaccounts/cdykes/web.html>

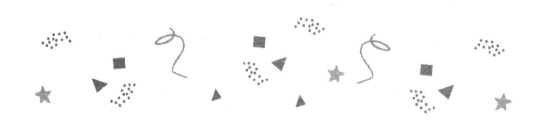

Celebrate Morse Code Day

Subject: Interdisciplinary

Grade level: 4 to 5

Celebrate May 24 (1844) as the day the first message in Morse Code was sent by Samuel F. B. Morse. The message "What hath God wrought!" was sent by telegraph from Washington, D.C. to Baltimore, Maryland.

Activity Title:
"Dah Dit"

Materials:

Web site access, books on the topic

Procedure:

Samuel Morse created a system of communication by understanding that pulses of electrical current carry information over wires. Amateur radio operators used Morse Code to send messages all over the world similar to how we use e-mail today. Boy Scouts still learn Morse Code.

Have your student understand this form of communication by using a printed page of Morse Code or the Morse Code translator (on the Boy Scout Web page) to "encrypt" a message to another student.

Evaluation:

Students will learn about Morse Code and communicate with another student.

Resources:

Morse Code Alphabet
 <http://www.soton.ac.uk/~scp93ch/morse/>
Boy Scouts of America: Morse Code Translator
 <http://www.bsa.scouting.org/fun/morse/>

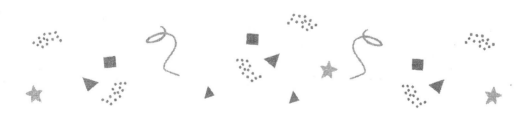

Celebrate National Physical Fitness and Sports Month

Subject: Physical Education, Math

Grade level: 5

Team up with the physical education teacher to plan the annual field day.

Activity Title:
Be Fit!

Materials:
Web site access

Procedure:
May is also Better Sleep Month! Have the students chart the number of hours of sleep they get each night. Who gets the least sleep? Probably the teacher!

Plan the field day activities with the physical education teacher. Students can use the computer to create a schedule of events for the school field events. Work with the physical education teacher to find some great lessons and activities ideas at PE Central's Web site.

Evaluation:
Students will learn about planning to be physically fit.

Resources:
PE Central
    <http://www.pecentral.org/>

Activity 71:
Celebrate Memorial Day

Subject: Social Studies
Grade level: 4 to 5

Memorial Day is celebrated on the last Monday in May. Examine the history and celebration of this yearly event.

Activity Title:
Remembrance

Materials:

Web site access, student journals

Procedure:

Have students research the beginnings of "Decoration Day," which began after the Civil War. Their research should reflect their understanding that on Memorial Day, we honor all those who gave their lives in service to their country.

Students also should find out about the celebration of this holiday in their own town or city, and create a list of what ceremonies will take place.

Evaluation:

Students will learn about the beginnings of this national holiday and how it is celebrated in their town or city.

Resources:

Noble: Memorial Day
<http://www.noblenet.org/year/tty5mem.htm>

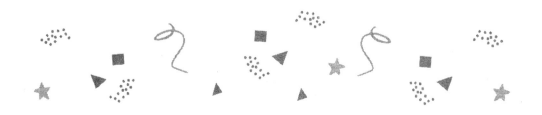

Celebrate National Creativity Month

Subject: Art

Grade level: K to 5

> Celebrate the creativity within all of us by enjoying some fresh lesson ideas using an existing classroom tool-the crayon.

Activity Title:
Creative Crayons

Materials:

Crayons, drawing paper, Web site access

Procedure:

Provide students with access to crayons and drawing paper to see what they can produce without prompting. Play music during this time. All students can enjoy working with the simple mediums of crayons and paper.

Teachers can browse the Crayola Web site to find lesson plans to match instructional goals to be used for the next school year's lessons or to be used as suggestions to parents for summer ideas. The Web is full of pages that can be printed and colored!

Evaluation:

Students will have the opportunity for free drawing time with crayons.

Resources:

Woods, Samuel. *Crayons from Start to Finish.* Woodbridge, CT: Blackbirch Press, 1999.
Crayola's Web Page for Education
<http://www.crayola.com/educators/lessons/>

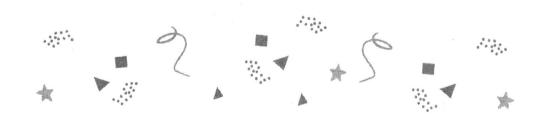

❖ June ❖

Activity 73:

Celebrate Field Trip Month

Subject: Interdisciplinary

Grade level: K to 5

Celebrate the end of the school year with a curriculum-related field trip. The ideal trip is to explore a museum or local site of historical or scientific interest. If that is not possible, why not try a virtual field trip using the Web? It still requires connection to your curriculum, planning, and implementing, but at least there are no soggy lunch bags, lost jackets, or sunburn!

Activity Title:
The Virtual Field Trip

Materials:
Web access, school district's acceptable use policy, snacks and drinks to be served outdoors if possible

Procedure:
Explore the Web resources for a trip with connections matched to your curriculum. Remember some of these trips may enrich or enhance experiences already taught during the school year. Review the school district's acceptable use policy, making sure you are following the guidelines.

Book the time for the virtual trip in the school computer lab. Notify the administration of this special event and ask for assistance from the classroom parents.

Check the chosen Web site for a few days prior to the experience to make sure it will function well during the "trip." Look for teacher or educator resources to help guide your lesson. If you have questions, e-mail the Webmaster of the site.

Decide which sections of the trip your students will be able to complete in the amount of time you have. You may want to determine the readability of the text to make sure your students can follow along independently. Prepare a worksheet as a guide for information gathering.

See if you may need special multimedia plug-ins. Test the chosen Web pages in the computer lab. Bookmark or make a favorite of the Web site's address at each computer.
Plan a wrap-up discussion in the classroom after a snack and drinks served outside.

Evaluation:
Students will gain real-life experiences by seeing how what they learn has application to work and study in adult life.

Resources:
Let's Plan a Field Trip
    <http://www.sdhc.k12.fl.us/~social.elementary/fieldtrips.htm>
Virtual Field Trips and Web Museums
    <http://www.midgefrazel.net/fieldtrip.html>

Celebrate Zoo and Aquarium Month

Subject: Interdisciplinary

Grade level: K to 5

Continue the field trip experience with National Zoo and Aquarium Month. If you can't schedule a real visit, then try watching zoo and aquarium life on the Web.

Activity Title:
Watching with Web Cams

Materials:

Web site access

Procedure:

Web cams can give students a view of the world by using the Internet. A camera is set up and focused on a resource and left on twenty-four hours a day. The live pictures are sent to you via the Internet. It is best to have a fast connection to the Web for this activity.

Bookmark sites with Web cams of marine mammals.

Evaluation:

Students will observe zoo and aquarium animals over the Web by learning about Web cameras.

Resources:

Aquaria/Zoos/Museum Resources
    <http://www.neaq.org/explore/air/aqua.html>
EarthCam for Kids (looks for zoos and aquariums)
    <http://www.earthcamforkids.com>
The National Zoo (look for ZooTV)
    <http://natzoo.si.edu/>

Activity 75:

Celebrate World Oceans Day

Subject: Science

Grade level: K to 5

Students have a fascination for the mysteries of oceans and ocean life. As you teach this topic and upon completion of your lessons or unit, use this simple game to reinforce the concepts learned. Celebrate World Oceans Day, an international celebration, held during the first week of June.

Activity Title:

"Who Am I? What Am I?" Game by Kathleen Wasik

Materials:

Pocket folders, handouts on sea life, ocean life reward stickers, field guides

Procedure:

Plan a lesson on sea creatures. If you don't live near an ocean, you can choose some common creatures of the Atlantic or Pacific Ocean from books and field guides in the library. There are many Web sites on sea life.

Prepare student handouts on the ocean life and reproduce them. If possible, plan a trip to the ocean or a local aquarium to see the ocean life in natural surroundings. As the students learn about each creature, place the handouts in their folder.

Generate clues for the game from the information learned by saying, "Who am I, what am I?" Then ask the question. Example: "I can make my stomach come right out of my body. I have five arms. If I lose one, I can grow another. Who am I?" (Answer: starfish) The game can be played to summarize for the day or as an activator for the next lesson.

Once a student has answered successfully, place an ocean life sticker on his or her folder.

Evaluation:

Students will be able to answer questions about our oceans and the creatures in them.

Resources:

Pledger, Maurice. *By the Seashore*. New York: Silver Dolphin, 1998.
World Oceans Day (background for the teacher)
    <http://www.panda.org/resources/publications/water/oceanday/>
The Field Trips Site: Oceans
    <http://www.field-guides.com/sci/oceank/index.htm>
Under the Sea: Thematic Unit on Marine Biology
    <http://www.geocities.com/sseagraves/underthesea.htm>

Celebrate Best Friends Day

Subject: Language Arts

Grade level: 2 to 5

> Finding a special friend who shares your interests, laughs at your jokes, and listens to your troubles is a lifelong reason to celebrate friends. June is a great month to record the friendships of the school year.

Activity Title:

Best Friend by Kathleen Wasik

Materials:

Digital or disposable camera, Reproducible Activity 76: Characteristics Graphic Organizer, pencils, writing paper, construction paper, whiteboard

Procedure:

Explain to the students that they are going to write the qualities of their best friends.

Brainstorm a list on the board of the qualities of a best friend, separating the outside qualities and inside qualities.

Take photographs of the students in your class with their best friend.

Pass out the photographs and Reproducible Activity 76: Characteristics Graphic Organizer to each student.

Using the graphic organizers, have the students make their own lists regarding their friends, making sure to separate the outside descriptions from the inside descriptions.

The students will use the graphic organizer as a resource for information when they begin to write. Students will write a paragraph or more, depending on age and ability, describing their friend.

Mount the pictures and the finished copies of descriptions on construction paper and display on the bulletin board.

Evaluation:

Students will write descriptions of their best friend, stating the friend's outside description, inside qualities, and the qualities that make the friend special.

Resources:

ALFY's Friendship Theme
   <http://www.alfy.com/teachers/teach/thematic_units/Friendship/Friendship_1.asp>

Activity 76: Characteristics Graphic Organizer

Name _____

Inside	Outside

Name _____

Inside	Outside

Celebrate National Juggling Day

Subject: Physical Education

Grade level: 4 to 5

National Juggling Day is celebrated on June 13 and makes a great June indoor or outdoor activity. It is fun, noncompetitive, and doesn't require a lot of equipment.

Activity Title:
Join the Circus

Materials:

Tennis balls, scarves

Procedure:

Start students by juggling two balls in an X pattern. If students find ball juggling frustrating, have them try scarf juggling instead.

Evaluation:

Students will learn to improve hand-eye coordination through simple juggling.

Resources:

Besmehn, Betty. *Juggling Step-by-Step*. New York: Sterling Publishing Co., 1994.
Juggling Information Service
    <http://www.juggling.org>
Debbie's Chinese Juggling Sticks
    <http://www.kidsdomain.com/craft/debstick.html>

Activity 78:

Celebrate Flag Day

Subject: Interdisciplinary

Grade level: K to 5

June 14 is Flag Day. This activity is a great way to wrap up the social studies celebrations found in this book and to connect to the patriotic celebrations of the summer.

Activity Title:

Respect Our Flag

Materials:

Biography of Betsy Ross, classroom flag, Web site access

Procedure:

Assign a team of students to learn about Betsy Ross, flag etiquette, and the evolution of our flag's history. These students can make an informal presentation to the class.

If some of your students are Boy or Girl Scouts, they may have experience with flags. They might like to wear their uniforms to school and demonstrate proper flag procedures learned in their troops.

Evaluation:

Students will learn about the history of our flag and the rules for respecting the flag.

Resources:

Wallner, Elizabeth. *Betsy Ross*. New York: Holiday House, 1994.
The Betsy Ross Homepage
    <http://www.ushistory.org/betsy/>
U.S. State Flag Quiz and Printouts
    <http://www.enchantedlearning.com/usa/flags/>

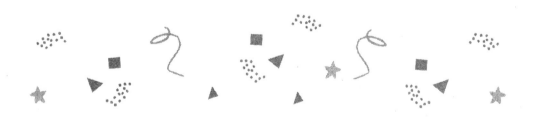

Activity 79:

Celebrate National Dairy Month

Subject: Health

Grade level: K to 5

Celebrate June's National Dairy Month by learning about dairy products and their relationship to summer activities.

Activity Title:
Strong Bones

Materials:

Whiteboard, Web site access

Procedure:

Brainstorm with the class the different kinds of dairy foods available for a healthy life. Which vitamins and minerals are contained in these foods? Which foods have the highest calorie count?

If your students are older, explain bone loss in older people and the role calcium takes to help prevent this.

Evaluation:

Students will learn about dairy products and their relationship to growing strong bones.

Resources:

National Dairy Month Fast Facts
    <http://www.fsa.usda.gov/pas/fsanews/html/2000/jun2000/factdairyalt.htm>
June Is Dairy Month
    <http://www.ca.uky.edu/carroll/home/f&cshealth.htm>

Celebrate Fireworks Safety Month

Subject: Interdisciplinary

Grade level: 3 to 5

Going to the fireworks is a favorite summertime activity. Celebrate Fireworks Safety Month that is celebrated from June 1 to July 4.

Activity Title:

Sparklers!

Materials:

Web site access

Procedure:

As a whole-class activity, survey the students to see if they attend a local fireworks display on the Fourth of July. Brainstorm with them some general safety rules. If you have Web site access, visit the National Council on Fireworks Safety and print the quiz and answers. Review the laws for your state.

Students can create posters about fireworks safety to be posted in the school cafeteria or library media center for the rest of the school to view.

Evaluation:

Students will learn about fireworks safety.

Resources:

National Council on Fireworks Safety
    <http://www.fireworksafety.com/classroom/index.html>
Federal and State Fireworks Regulations
    <http://www.cpsc.gov/cpscpub/pubs/july4/regs.html>
4th of July Fireworks Safety
    <http://www.usacitylink.com//usa/?file=/citylink/usa/safety.html>

Activity 81:
Celebrate Father's Day

Subject: Art, Language Arts

Grade level: 2 to 5

> Father's Day has been celebrated in the United States since 1910, but it was not an official national holiday until 1972.

Activity Title:
Design a Tie

Materials:

Art supplies, white writing paper, Web site access

Procedure:

To celebrate this day, have students design a paper tie for a special male family member (father, stepfather, foster father, grandfather, brother, uncle) and write a paragraph on the back of the tie explaining how this person has been influential in their life. This tie and writing activity also can be designed as a card.

Evaluation:

Students will design a special Father's Day tie.

Resources:

Father's Day
    <http://www.unkc.edu/imc/fathers.htm>
EnchantedLearning.com: Tie Card
    <http://www.enchantedlearning.com/crafts/cards/tie/>

Celebrate the Last Day of School

Subject: Reading, Art

Grade level: K to 5

The last day of school is a great day to encourage summer reading by your students. Your school district may have a summer reading list, and your local public library may participate in a summer reading program.

Activity Title:

Summer!

Materials:

Art supplies, bookmark printouts, light tag, laminating materials

Procedure:

Have the students design their own bookmarks for their summer reading and to place in their journal to end the writing activities for the school year.

If Web site access is available, take a look at the Vacation Memory Book as a last day activity.

Visit the local public library to find out if the town or city participates in a summer reading program, and send that information home to parents.

Evaluation:

Students will be encouraged to read throughout the summer months and develop this lifelong habit.

Resources:

EnchantedLearning.com Vacation Memory Book
    <http://www.enchantedlearning.com/crafts/books/vacationmemory/>

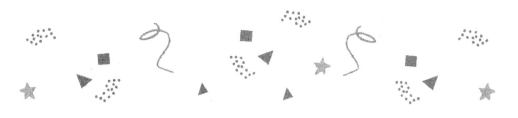

Celebrate Vacation Days: Nature Journal

Subject: Science, Reading

Grade level: 1 to 5

> Encourage continued use of the student journals by giving your students some ideas for using journals in a nonschool setting. Naturalists use journals to record observations about the flora and fauna of the natural world.

Activity Title:
Go Outside and Observe

Materials:

Student journals, plastic magnifying glasses, Reproducible Activity 83: Nature Journal

Procedure:

Students are naturally curious about nature. Help them use their student journals to record observations of plants and animals outdoors. Use Reproducible Activity 83: Nature Journal to brainstorm headings for recording observations. Younger students may need parental guidance with this type of summer activity.

Evaluation:

Students will learn how naturalists use journals to record observations.

Resources:

Field guides for students at the library

Activity 83: Nature Journal

Celebrate Vacation Days:
Word-a-Week Journal

Subject: Language Arts
Grade level: 2 to 5

Encourage continued use of the student journals to have students work on their vocabulary and handwriting during the summer.

Activity Title:
New Words

Materials:

List of new words appropriate for the student's grade level, dictionaries

Procedure:

Depending upon the grade level and reading ability of your class, create a list of words for students to look up and write in their journals. Older students might enjoy using the Web to find the definitions. Send home a list for the parents, along with suggestions for summer reading.

Evaluation:

Students will continue to learn new words and their definitions during vacation, and record them in their journal.

Resources:

School spelling workbooks, word-a-day calendars for kids

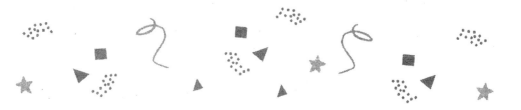

Celebrate Vacation Days:
New Faces, New Places

Subject: Social Studies, Language Arts

Grade level: 1 to 5

> Encourage continued use of the student journals by having students record the names of new people they meet during the summer and new places they visit.

Activity Title:
Places and People

Materials:

Student journals, pencils

Procedure:

Students have new experiences beyond the classroom. Have the students think about what they will be doing during the summer months. Even if they have no specific plans, exciting people and places can be found right in their own neighborhood.

Evaluation:

Students will look beyond the classroom into their own community and lives for new experiences and new people.

Resources:

People in the neighborhood, people on vacation, places to visit near home and far away

Celebrate Vacation Days: Reflective Journaling

Subject: Creative writing

Grade level: 4 to 5

Encourage continued use of the student journals by having students write in their journals as a private diary.

Activity Title:
Dear Diary

Materials:

Student journals

Procedure:

Journals used in the classroom are not like private diaries. Many nonfiction diaries are written "to the diary." These reflective entries are not meant to be read by other people. Some past diaries have become an important part of history. Respect for privacy is an important lesson for your older students to begin learning.

Evaluation:

Students will learn about journaling as a measure of personal reflection.

Resources:

Blank books, simple notebooks, examples of diaries

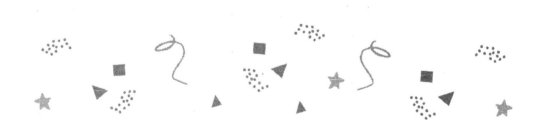

Celebrate Vacation Days: Back to School Supplies

Subject: Reading, Math

Grade level: 1 to 5

Many school districts have a list of required school supplies to be purchased for the student to use for the next school year. Win the hearts of busy parents by providing a list for them to use when shopping during the summer.

Activity Title:
Supplies for Learning

Materials:

List of school supplies for the student for the next grade

Procedure:

At the end of July, barely a month after some schools close their doors for the summer, stores start putting newly stocked school supplies on their shelves. Busy parents and their pocketbooks would appreciate a basic list of school supplies sent home at the end of the school year instead of in the rush of the first days of school in August or September. Have students staple this inside their journals for summer shopping. Encourage the school district to place this list on their Web site.

Evaluation

Students will learn the value of being prepared for the next school year.

Resources:

Classroom or school district's list of required or suggested school supplies

❖ Bibliography ❖

Print Resources

Chase's Calendar of Events. 2001 ed. Chicago: Contemporary Books, 2001.

Cohen, Hennig, and Tristram Potter Coffin, eds. *The Folklore of American Holidays.* 3rd ed. Detroit: Gale Group, 1999.

Dunkling, Leslie. *A Dictionary of Days.* New York: Facts on File Publications, 1988.

Haglund, Elaine J., and Marcia L. Harris. *On This Day: A Collection of Everyday Learning Events and Activities for the Media Center, Library and Classroom.* Littleton: Libraries Unlimited, Inc., 1983.

Henderson, Helene, and Ellen Thompson, eds. Holidays, *Festivals and Celebrations of the World.* Detroit: Omnigraphics, Inc., 1997.

Macmillan Profiles: Festivals and Holidays. New York: Macmillan Library Reference USA, 1999.

Simpson, Carol. *Daily Journals.* Parsippany, NJ: Good Year Books, 1993.

Web Sites

Classroom Connect's Connected Teacher Calendar. 15 Sept. 2001 <http://www1.classroom.com/community/connection/calendar.jhtml>.

History Channel's This Day in History. 15 Sept. 2001 <http://www.historychannel.com/thisday/>.

The Holiday Zone. 15 Sept. 2001 <http://www.theholidayzone.com/>.

Infoplease.com Daily Almanac. 15 Sept. 2001 <http://ln.infoplease.com/cgi-bin/daily>.

NOBLE (North of Boston Library Exchange) Web: Through the Year. 15 Sept. 2001 <http://www.noblenet.org/year/>.

Wilstar's Holiday Page. 15 Sept. 2001 <http://wilstar.com/holidays/>.

Worldwide Holiday and Festival Site. 15 Sept. 2001 <http://www.holidayfestival.com/>.

Yahoo: Holidays and Observances. 15 Sept. 2001 <http://dir.yahoo.com/Society_and_Culture/holidays_and_observances/>.

Yahooligan's This Day in History. 15 Sept. 2001 <http://www.yahooligans.com/docs/tdih/>.

❖ Index ❖

Printed in the USA
CPSIA information can be obtained
at www.ICGtesting.com
LVHW080723170724
785510LV00007B/269

9 781586 831073